SUPERVISION:
THE RELUCTANT PROFESSION

SUPERVISION:

THE RELUCTANT

PROFESSION

RALPH L. MOSHER AND DAVID E. PURPEL

Graduate School of Education
Harvard University

with the assistance of

KIYO MORIMOTO

Bureau of Study Counsel
Harvard University

HOUGHTON MIFFLIN COMPANY • BOSTON

NEW YORK • ATLANTA • GENEVA, ILL. • DALLAS • PALO ALTO

Printed in the U.S.A.

Library of Congress Catalog Card Number: 72-158636

ISBN: 0-395-12509-X

FOREWORD

Perhaps the most significant thing about this book is that its authors truly comprehend the importance of supervision; they have, as a result, committed themselves to a profoundly searching study. They have pondered the existing evidence on what supervision has meant until now, what it has tried to do and how well it has worked. Driven to the honest conclusion that it has rarely had much success, they have simply refused to stop, because they know we *must* develop a system of supervision that *does* work. There is too much at stake to allow us not to.

Most directly at stake is the ability of our teachers to teach effectively. That demands mastery of technique—suggesting that we had better stop apologizing for the craft of pedagogy —and, perhaps even more, a quality of human relationship whose source is the person inside the teacher. But even more fundamentally at issue is the curriculum itself, the program of the school and its very purposes. If, as a profession, we are unable to diagnose, plan and act at this level, we are done for.

It is the special quality of *Supervision: The Reluctant Profession* that its authors grasp the full range of essential demands—not just one or two fragments—and have stretched their minds to find whole answers. They have not found all those answers yet—no one has—but they are willing to consider all the variables, to analyze a massive volume of research and to test their products against rigorous standards in their own working situations.

Thus, they have a deep respect for competence in the classroom, for the art and the craft of practical pedagogy. They are willing to speak bluntly of "trying to educate teachers about the curriculum and how to teach it." They have struggled to develop a style of supervision that will genuinely help a teacher teach with greater skill. And they are aware of the great benefits to be gained from videotaping, interaction analysis and other modern means of analyzing the act of teaching.

Yet, at the same time, they are deeply aware that what the teacher is as a person, and how he relates with those he teaches, is more important than even the best "methods."

Therefore, they have explored carefully the possibilities inherent in the sophisticated use of counseling technique and of modern group work.

Finally, they know that the school is a huge and hard-to-change institution with a tremendous social responsibility. Supervision cannot possibly be considered adequate unless it also offers *leadership* in building the structures, conditions and, above all, the curricula our times demand.

None of these great themes can be treated exhaustively in one short book, but the writers have probed each one honestly. In the first two chapters they stipulate their definitions with unusual diligence, and build a careful background of philosophical values and pragmatic observations. In the third chapter they set down what may well be the best existing interpretation of the research on teacher effectiveness and supervision. (Though this chapter focuses specifically on research, the running bibliographical notes throughout the book would make an admirable guide to the study of supervision.)

Chapters Four to Seven, the heart of the book, are devoted to various actual procedures of supervision. Chapter Four approaches them in a general, preliminary way and wrestles with issues generic to supervision, regardless of method. Chapter Five concentrates on "clinical supervision," which the reader may well see as traditional, analytical observation and consultation at their modern best. The chapter is rich in specific detail. Chapters Six and Seven shift to a more "psychological" orientation, whose primary concern is the teacher-as-person. The first of these chapters focuses on individual work through ego-counseling; in the second the emphasis is on the use of a group which limits its attention to *professional* problems of teaching and learning, but nonetheless echoes the more personally-oriented processes of encounter groups, T-groups and the like.

In none of these chapters is there any attempt to "sell" a particular approach as "*the* way." One feels, rather, that the writers are probing a huge problem to see how much it may be solved in one way, how much in another. And this is particularly true of the final chapter, where the tremendous problems of institutional adaptation are defined far more precisely than is any solution.

This is, in other words, a book for readers who are willing to face up to great challenges and speculate boldly about solutions. A book for the real student. It is a *modern* book, rejecting a good deal of the outworn conventional wisdom and opting pretty consistently for more sophisticated and, therefore, often more complex lines of solution consonant both with recent research and with the spirit of human relationships in our times. It provides a good deal of realistic and detailed procedural guidance, and yet its greatest strength is its fine analysis of problems and possibilities.

Supervision has fallen on hard times in recent years. Even if old-style supervision had been much more effective than it was, it would today be unsuited to our patterns of relating. We have valuable new resources and insights at our disposal. They need to be used. If supervision is to gain real leverage—and I believe this to be essential to the actualization of education's potential—it will be through such bold, honest, pioneering efforts as Professors Mosher and Purpel have made in this book.

Fred T. Wilhelms
Senior Associate
Association for Supervision and
Curriculum Development

INTRODUCTION

This book reflects the writers' personal and professional careers over the past 15 years. That odyssey has included training elementary school teachers in depressed mining towns in Cape Breton; supervising Harvard Master of Arts in Teaching candidates in a wide variety of public schools; training independent school headmasters in contexts ranging from the magisterial to the *noveau riche*, and struggling, with graduate students and colleagues at Harvard, to clarify what we mean by supervision. During this 15-year span we have taught courses in education, supervised in the field, administered teacher education programs and counseled teachers. The central focus of these efforts has always been *the education of teachers* for their work in the classroom. That experience and that priority permeate this book.

The book also reflects a belief that our reluctant profession needs most of all a range of ideas and practices for the supervision of teachers. We do not arrive at this position theoretically. Indeed, what we know about supervision derives primarily from practice. The complexity of teaching and teachers simply will not yield to any single concept or practice of supervision. If we have a single bone to pick with our reluctant profession, it is with those people who look for, or offer, single or simplistic prescriptions for educating teachers. The writers have acted on all of the ideas set forth in this book, and we know they are not enough. But they are something. In particular, they represent our efforts at the hard thinking and hard practice which we believe *can* bring about progress in this field.

The book is divided, invisibly but undeniably, into three parts. The first part—Chapters One through Four—is background. Chapter One offers working definitions of supervision and teaching, and an overview of the book's central themes. Chapter Two surveys the historical origins of supervision and discusses traditional philosophical stances toward it, notably "scientific' supervision, which emphasizes careful empirical research and administrative efficiency, and "democratic" supervision, which stresses teacher autonomy and talent. The chapter goes on to identify traditional functions of supervision and factors which have deterred the development of vigorous supervisory programs in the public schools. Chapter Three is a survey of current research on teaching and supervision, intended to familiarize the reader with what is currently "known" about both. Chapter Four offers a conceptual framework for the educational and social responsibilities of supervision, and enumerates the personal, social and cognitive skills we feel are necessary to undertake these responsibilities effectively.

Chapters Five through Seven each discuss in detail a particular method of supervision, giving considerable attention to both theory and technique. Supervisory techniques are too often discussed in a vacuum, without theoretical support or validation. We feel that the conceptual bases of the supervisory methods under discussion are fully as important to the field as are the accompanying recommendations for practice. Specifics, however, are not slighted—effective supervision, like effective teaching, requires a wide repertoire of instructional methods, some quite complex. Chapter Five describes a supervisory program which has tried to put into practice the values and assumptions implicit in traditional models of supervision. Chapter Six deals with the implications for supervision of counseling theory and technique. We assume that what the teacher *is personally* affects how he teaches and what pupils learn, and believe strongly that supervision must develop ways to respond to the teacher as a person and as an autonomous professional. A method based on counseling theory and technique is outlined in considerable detail. Chapter Seven, "Supervising Teachers in Groups," by our colleague Kiyo Morimoto, also focuses on the teacher's personal development, but in the context of a group rather than an individual conference. The chapter discusses the composition and characteristics of such groups, the process by which teachers learn about themselves and methods suitable for facilitating such learning.

Chapter Eight represents the book's final section. It calls for supervision to reassert vigorous leadership in reformulating the content and methods of education, outlines a new role for supervisors and suggests some new directions for curriculum innovation. It is in this area of educational leadership that supervision has been most reluctant. The need for alternative forms of education is critical, yet it is only black parents, a few independent schools and radical educators who respond. Obviously it is easier to criticize existing schools than to propose alternatives. Yet on both issues supervision has been conspicuously silent. In this challenge lies, we believe, the ultimate test of whether supervision will remain a very proper and very perennial bridesmaid. The writers have no illusions that this book is, or could be, a definitive answer. But, under any circumstances, a book cannot transcend its essential subject matter. What we have tried to do is to recognize the problems facing supervision, to ask hard questions and to offer some examined practices which suggest one way out of reluctance. That, we hope, is a contribution to leadership.

Ralph L. Mosher
and
David E. Purpel

CONTENTS

CHAPTER ONE

DEFINITIONS AND DIRECTIONS

Despite the numberless speeches, textbooks and journal articles devoted to discussion of supervision in elementary and secondary schools, many educators still wonder whether there really *is* such a thing as "supervision" and are puzzled at the widespread concern—attested to by the appearance of yet another book—about such an elusive concept. One of the most frequent statements we hear about supervision is "in our school we don't have any." And even if we assume that supervision is an identifiable entity, there remain conflicting definitions and attitudes toward it within the teaching profession. Supervision has been variously defined as the improvement of instruction, teacher development, curriculum leadership and school administration.[1] Differences of opinion

[1]The variety of proposed definitions of supervision is reflected in a sample of titles in this field: Edmund Amidon and Elizabeth Hunter, *Improving Teaching: The Analysis of Classroom Verbal Interaction;* John Adolph Bartky, *Supervision as Human Relations* (Boston: D. C. Heath & Company, 1953); W. H. Burton and L. J. Brueckner, *Supervision: A Social Process* (New York: Appleton-Century-Crofts, 1955), and Jane Franseth, *Supervision as Leadership* (Evanston: Row Peterson, 1961).

exist not only about the objectives of supervision but also about the way it should be undertaken. The long-standing conflict in this field between "scientific" and "democratic" supervision, to be discussed later, is an example of such a controversy. Though lip service is routinely paid to the importance of supervision, the most widespread attitude is probably suspicion—suspicion that supervision is at best ineffectual and at worst a harmful form of interference with the work of the teacher. By and large, educators are confused in their understanding of supervision and ambivalent in their feelings about it.

SUPERVISION: DEFINITIONS

The concept of supervision is a simple one, describing a process common to all professions and occupations. The supervisor is charged with making certain that another person does a good job. Sergeants exist to insure that those under their command are good soldiers; football coaches are supposed to make sure that their teams win games, and foremen see that assembly workers turn the right screws in the right ways. In such clear-cut situations, the purpose and methods of supervision are self-evident: a good job is instantly recognizable as such when it is achieved. (As Vince Lombardi said: "Winning is the only thing.") So too is the level of worker expertise needed to achieve the desired goal. When, however, we try to apply this simple notion of supervision to the profession of teaching, where objectives are less explicit and skills less precisely measurable, things become considerably more confused.

The conflicting pressures on the school supervisor to teach; to work with student teachers and beginning teachers and to evaluate experienced teachers; to supervise across subject areas; to direct curriculum projects, and to discharge a host of administrative and clerical tasks, complicate the problem of defining the job. It almost becomes the case that supervision in schools is most accurately defined as what the particular supervisor does or says he does.

The difficulty of defining supervision in relation to education also stems, in large part, from unsolved theoretical problems about teaching. Quite simply, we lack sufficient understanding of the process of teaching. Our theories of learning are inadequate, the criteria for measuring teaching effectiveness are imprecise, and deep disagreement exists about what knowledge—that is, what curriculum—is most valuable to teach. There is no generally agreed-upon definition of what teaching is or of how to measure its effects. The systematic improvement of instruction, and clarification of the place and practice of supervision in such improvement, must ultimately wait upon basic research on questions of this kind. When we have achieved more understanding of *what* and *how* to teach, and with what *special effects* on students, we will be much less vague about the supervision of these processes.

We must, in the meantime, adopt operational definitions of supervision and of teaching which are sufficiently flexible to allow us to work usefully toward the eventual clarification of both processes. Because we believe that there is currently no "right" view of supervision, we have agreed upon a two-pronged definition which reflects our view of what supervisors should do. We consider the tasks of supervision to be *teaching teachers how to teach (in which working with teachers as people is a significant subfunction), and professional leadership in reformulating public education—more specifically, its curriculum, its teaching and its forms.* Others have, of course, defined supervision differently, as, for example, the administration of instruction or the administrative and personnel reorganization of schools, but we believe the most significant conception of supervision is incorporated in our definition.

PRACTICAL PEDAGOGY

Considerable support can be found in the literature for a definition of supervision as "effecting the improvement of classroom instruction." If one of the basic purposes of the school is formal instruction, it is a prime function of supervision (particularly as it has developed historically) to improve the quality of that instruction. When supervision is concerned with what is taught, how it is taught, and with the effects of teaching on the learner, it is itself a special kind of teaching, involving a unique set of students (called teachers) and a unique content (called curriculum). The term "supervisor" in this context describes a teacher who is deliberately trying to educate classroom teachers about the curriculum and how to teach it. This suggests a relatively specific process: the systematic instruction of teachers in the implementation of a particular curriculum (for example, PSSC physics). Such a definition, seemingly restrictive and operational, nonetheless does not clarify how supervision differs in objective and functions from school administration or from teaching, or whether its content is in any respect different from curriculum. Subsequent chapters will deal with these issues in detail.

Working With Teachers as People

It is a crucial component in the process of teaching teachers, we believe, to work with teachers as people. Our reasoning is founded on the belief that what the teacher *is* personally affects what he does, how he teaches and what the pupils do and learn. In order to improve classroom instruction, implement a curriculum or affect children's formal learning, the supervisor must take into account the powerful contributing effect of the teacher's personality and his relationship with the child. No less significant is the effect of the teacher's personality on the child's informal learning. Certainly one of the critical factors in determining the "potency" of a school is the personal qualities of the adults who participate in it.

Teachers, as people, exert an enormous influence on children's attitudes, self-concepts and sense of personal worth. Any educator knows this. It is harder for the profession to admit that teachers, as people, can blight as well as foster the personal growth of children. The writings of Rosenthal, Kohl, Holt, Silberman and others confirm the important truth of this observation. In this sense, every teacher is a "psychological educator." Many writers on education argue that the effects of this "hidden curriculum" (on poor children in city schools, for example) are more significant and harmful than is the program of formal education. Thus it is extremely important that supervision be able to understand and to respond to teachers as persons. Entire "schools" of supervision theory have developed around this broad question. But too frequently their prescriptions for supervision have been essentially ideological (i.e., advocating "democratic" supervision or supervision as "human relations"), rather than practical. We view the supervisor's work with the teacher as a person as a very subtle process, but a manageable and decidedly nonideological one.

LEADERSHIP IN THE REFORMULATION OF EDUCATION

It is a second major function of supervision to provide professional leadership in reformulating public education. By this we mean that supervision must contribute curriculum materials, a practical knowledge of pedagogy and new ideas and procedures for educating children better. The "curriculum," in simplest terms, is those experiences, materials and techniques that constitute what the students are supposed to and/or actually learn. It is both the intended educational program and what actually happens to the students as a result of their exposure to the program. We will use the term very broadly to designate traditional school subjects like history, reading and biology and, as well, programs designed to teach such things as character, physical fitness and manual dexterity. It is not enough for a supervisor to be very good at analyzing teaching or developing curriculum with teachers. Supervision, so delimited, is confronting only two—albeit crucial—aspects of education. In our view, the problems of public education are both sufficiently complex and sufficiently grave to require substantially more than improved classroom teaching and more mature teachers. Practical know-how, vision and ideas are all necessary to improve the educational system as a whole.

TEACHING: DEFINITIONS

Our working definition of teaching is comparably pragmatic. We make use of several definitions of teaching throughout this book, the particular formulation depending to some degree on the supervisory function being discussed. When discussing supervision as teaching teachers how to teach or as the analysis of classroom instruction, we define teaching simply as *what teachers do*. A "teacher," in the strictest generic sense, is someone who deliberately tries to persuade someone else to change his thinking or behavior in a specific direction. A variety of approaches may be used to this end, including clarification, analysis, force, bribery and seduction. These teaching approaches—be they rational, irrational or coercive—are aimed at changing people, i.e., "students," although the actual changes that occur in students as a result of these approaches can be (and often are) different from those intended. Notwithstanding the variety of methods available, teaching *as typically practiced* consists mainly of talk between the teacher and the students. As Smith and Meux succinctly state, "Teaching behavior is primarily verbal" (1959, p.129). Flanders, for example, has estimated that approximately two-thirds of classroom time in this country is spent by teachers talking to students (1964, pp. 196-231). Ways to analyze and affect this process are essential, then, if we want to improve how children are presently taught. But we also know that teaching is basically a social process involving talk and interaction between at least two people, a teacher and a student. This definition of teaching as a fundamentally social or interpersonal process is our basic rationale for arguing that supervisors work with teachers as people. If we combine these two definitions, the result is a model of a process sufficiently observable, sufficiently consistent, sufficiently typical of most classroom practice and sufficiently related to what children learn in school to be productively studied.

It would be tempting to stop here, but the definition is too limiting. For one thing, it still focuses on "teaching." Although in most schools, for most teachers and most students, teaching *is* the predominant means of instruction, it is still only one of a large number of possible ways of making learning possible. We believe that the crucial task facing education as a profession is *to recognize and to develop the full range of conditions under which people can be taught and/or learn.* We see supervision as contributing to this search. Clearly, it is not possible to define in advance what these new conceptions of education will be. We therefore put no definitional limits on this supervisory function, except to oppose education at the cost of systematic physical pain, humiliation or indoctrination. George Leonard's *Education and Ecstasy* (1968), for example, is unlikely to be considered a book about supervision. We think it is one. Leonard's ideas about affective and technologically-oriented education are examples of creative imagination applied to the forms education may take in the future. Alas, that kind of vision does not characterize textbooks on supervision (including this one). We regard such conceptualizing about education *plus* the research and development work necessary to make such visions concrete as the ultimate supervisory function.

THEMES

The implications of these operational definitions of supervision and teaching can be briefly illustrated by reference to some of the assumptions underlying our viewpoint and choices of emphasis. Perhaps the most fundamental is the issue of who the client of the supervision process is. Supervision serves the child and his learning as well as the larger community. Our concern with the process of teaching, with the curriculum, the teacher's development and the school itself derives in part, of course, from their complexity as variables in a process, and the need to study and understand their interaction both abstractly and in their concrete applications. But supervision's essential spirit and ethic derives from its obligation to provide optimal occasions for learning for the individual child.

Several other themes follow naturally. Throughout the book it is argued that what and how we teach our children needs careful review and basic improvement. Virtually all texts and theories of supervision say the same thing in one way or another. Where and when instruction is accomplished with less than optimal effect, improvement is necessary, and it would be difficult to argue that our schools currently offer many examples of optimal effect. Teachers are paid for their services and thus may justifiably be assessed and asked to modify practices which are found wanting. The protection of the client necessitates and justifies evaluation and requirements to modify teaching practices.

A view of the school as the focus and crucible of projected changes in education is also an inherent theme of this book. We view the school as an institution whose resources are unequal to its current task, to say nothing of the roles projected for it. The public school does not enjoy the institutional autonomy, the selectivity about who and what to teach or the intellectual and research resources of the university. It lacks the funding resources of government and industry's inducements to talent. What it does have is an enormous primary responsibility: the education of all children. It must respond to the most poignant hopes and aspirations of the parents of these children. It is expected, too, to remedy a remarkable range of social problems, which run the gamut from driver education to the effects of racial segregation. The school is expected to be an instrument of national objectives. Appropriately enough, it is continuously asked to reevaluate its basic educational values and policy. In brief, the school must respond to powerful, impinging forces for change. The recent extensive curriculum activity within the basic educational system (i.e., curriculum reform, organizational changes, the involvement of big business and of the federal government) is both a symptom and an augury of those forces.

It is essential that the school have the personnel and technical tools to effect significant improvement, *on its own terms*, of both curriculum and teaching. In our view, one of the basic jobs of the supervisor is to be a specialized practitioner, a curriculum and instructional leader within the school. No such specialty is currently applying its expertise to problems of curriculum and teaching generated by the school. The responsibilities discussed in this book as appropriate for the supervisor could strengthen the existing roles of the department chairman and the principal. Certainly there should be concern for splitting the managerial from the curriculum leadership responsibility of both the department chairman and the principal. Clearly, too, the functions we discuss provide additional ideas and practice for the supervision of both beginning and experienced teachers, a specialty for which there appears to be compelling present need (Edelfelt, 1966). The fundamental goal of the competencies we shall discuss, however, is to provide leadership personnel and capabilities in curriculum and instruction within the school. We assume that our educational system needs both external challenge and vigorous internal renewal. We do not believe that the aspirations of the public, the government, the universities or of schoolmen themselves for the educational system can be met realistically without personnel capable of substantial educational leadership within the school itself. Unless teachers accept this challenge and acquire skill in the analysis of the educational program, the children in the schools will continue to be short-changed.

We have become, over the last several years, increasingly concerned about the effects on children of the school, the curriculum and teaching and more radical and comprehensive in our vision of what must be done. The criticisms of Paul Goodman and Edgar Friedenberg; the accounts of the teaching experiences of Herbert Kohl and Jonathan Kozol; documentary films such as Frederick Wiseman's "High School" and the findings of the Coleman Report on the Equality of Educational Opportunity raise deeply troublesome questions about public education. Controversy over "community control" of the schools, divisive teacher strikes, student protests, the racial polarization in urban schools—and our experience of the creeping paralysis of the educational program in many of these schools—are other symptoms of malaise. The reader may find this a dark view, a realistic one, or both. We are not, however, "school is dead" theologians. We believe that public education is in trouble (deeply so in the city, subtly so in the suburbs), and this book is, in part, an assessment of how much must be done. Our confidence that it can be done is attested to by our decision to write this book.

Our views on the functions most crucial to supervision have been directly influenced by this vision of the educational system. By emphasizing personnel training, curriculum development and teacher development, we are saying that change in education is, to a significant degree, a matter of better trained teachers and better curriculum. To this end, a basic objective of supervision should be curricular and instructional leadership. If one acknowledges that most of our schools are still characterized by a static curriculum and unexamined teaching, this is in itself a radical goal. But, in another sense, it will remain essentially static if educational leadership is designed primarily to rationalize existing curricula and forms of teaching. Such leadership has the effect of strengthening the existing educational system. We believe there is a significant need and place for such leadership. Ninety-nine percent of American education takes place, after all, in "the existing educational system."

We are, however, willing to question whether such leadership is sufficient, given the profound deficiencies of, and substantial demands made on the schools. Whether educational engineers, even efficient ones, can transform the curriculum, the process and the context of education is a moot question. Technocrats rarely have visions, and without vision the children perish. Is supervision up to that challenge? We must concede that this book will not guarantee that supervision alone can make such a great leap forward. But questions of this order are perhaps more important than the immediate response of supervisors or of other schoolmen and writers of books on supervision. Indeed, raising them emphasizes the legitimacy and intellectual rigor of educational supervision, which otherwise might be in danger of qualifying as the second most dismal science.

CHAPTER TWO

THE TRADITION
AND THE CHALLENGE

The field of supervision has traditionally confronted a number of persistent and thorny problems whose source is the competing clienteles of the supervisor—society, teachers, schools and students. Supervisors are subject to the needs and demands of all of these groups and to the fundamental and complex questions that emerge from them. For example, who should define the proper objectives of the teacher? Does he work to satisfy the community? the school board? the superintendent? the principal? the department chairman? the university? himself? Is the teacher an autonomous, self-generating, well-trained professional who should have responsibility for determining what knowledge is to be taught and how? Or should the critically important and sensitive work of the teacher be supplemented by direction, guidance and assessment? Who protects the community and children from the incompetent or irresponsible teacher? To whom can teachers turn for assistance and guidance in improving their performance?

THE HISTORY AND TRADITIONS OF SUPERVISION

Books on supervision often approach these questions by chronicling the evolution of predominant practices or objectives of supervision. The reader will find useful and comprehensive chapters on the evolution of supervision in this country in Gwynn's *Theory and Practice of Supervision* (1961, pp. 3-19) and in Lucio and McNeil's *Supervision: A Synthesis of Thought and Action* (1962, pp. 3-21). Cremin's *The Transformation of the School* (1961), while it does not discuss supervision *per se*, is valuable for understanding the broad educational forces at work in the evolution of supervision. All of this material suggests that supervision originated as inspection of schools, and that this remained its major emphasis until about 1920. Lucio and McNeil say that "supervision has no independent thought of its own" (1962, p. 11). It is also evident that supervision began with no identity of its own, as an adjunct of school administration. Local and district superintendents had to delegate responsibility for administration and inspection as the public schools expanded and became more specialized in their curriculum and staffing at the end of the nineteenth century. Historically, too, supervision in the public schools has been the simultaneous ward of many institutions: the school board, the superintendency, state normal schools, state departments of education, state universities and regional college accrediting associations. The history of supervision reveals surprisingly exact precedents for the muddy contemporary definitions of supervision summarized in Chapter One. In this sense, to read about supervision in 1920 is to read about supervision in 1970. It is also clear that supervision grew and took on new functions in a rather haphazard way. For example, "the improvement of instruction" and "course of study construction" were widely recognized as major objectives of supervision by 1920 (Gwynn 1961, p. 9).

The next stage in the growth of this field, which lasted

from about 1920 to 1950, produced two major theories of supervision which still maintain influence and vitality. (As Lucio and McNeil note, "The similarity between the educational views of leaders in the early scientific movement and the views of persons currently doing research with autoinstructional materials is striking" (1962, p. 10). These are the traditions of "scientific" and "democratic" supervision.

SCIENTIFIC SUPERVISION

The scientific approach to supervision emphasizes careful empirical research and administrative efficiency. These values, in effect, represent faith in the possibility of objectively measuring critical behavior related to effective teaching, and imply an assumption that teaching behavior can be carefully controlled and regulated for optimal operation. Scientific supervision has spawned vast numbers of empirical questionnaires and analytical studies, all designed to produce a science of teaching. Supervisors who operate in this tradition see it as their job to encourage and conduct research and to interpret the findings to teachers as a basis for improving their teaching. In addition to the importance of research, there is emphasis on efficient administration and tight organization. These practices, which originated in the scientific management of industry, are regarded as a means of bringing economy, order and stability to the schools. A significant characteristic of the efficiency-oriented theory of administration is the importance placed on hierarchy, organization and evaluation—critical values in any institution bent on "efficiency" and "productivity."

Lucio and McNeil have described this approach lucidly and succinctly:

Scientific management proposed to alter the personal relations between supervisors and teachers. Instead of the supervisors directing the methods of the teachers in a personal and arbitrary manner, . . .

the primary task of the scientific supervisor was to discover educational "laws" and apply them through the labors of the teacher. The teacher would be expected to find the controlling law through cooperation with the supervisor. Neither was to be personally over the other, for both were under the law of science . . .

It was the supervisory staff which was to have the largest share in the work of determining proper methods. The burden of finding the best methods was too great and too complex to be laid on the shoulders of teachers. The teacher was expected to be a specialist in the practice that would produce the "product"; the supervisor was to specialize in the science relating to the process. Supervisors were to (1) discover best procedures in the performance of particular tasks and (2) give these best methods to the teachers for their guidance (1962, p. 8).

DEMOCRATIC SUPERVISION

Democratic supervision, which has its roots in the Progressive education tradition, emphasizes the dignity of the individual teacher. It originated, in part, as a reaction to the previous predominance of the inspection and evaluation function in administration and supervision. (Democratic supervision implicitly still wars against this earlier tradition. The image of the supervisor as a person whose main job is to suppress individual creativity, create fear and conformity and fire imaginative teachers seems to have remarkable emotional longevity in the profession.) Democratic supervision was also influenced by a parallel movement in progressive education. Guidance, defined as vocational and educational counseling leading to wise occupational choice, greater individual fulfillment and "the creation of a more efficient and humane industrial system," became a significant new educational ideology in the period 1910–1920 (Cremin 1965, p. 5). As seems to be true of many innovations in education, a practice devised for students was soon applied to teachers as well. Supervision began to be conceived of as guidance. Kyte defined supervision in 1930 as "the maximum development of the teacher into the most professionally efficient person she is capable of becoming" (1930, p. 45).

The interested reader is referred to Lucio and McNeil (1962) for discussion of other influences on the tradition of democratic supervision in the 1930's and 1940's. Sufficient for our purposes is their statement that "supervision became associated with precepts respecting human personality and encouraging wide participation in the formulation of policy" (p. 11). We can thus summarize the basic principles of democratic supervision:

1. The integrity of the individual teacher must be protected and upheld at all times.

2. Supervision should be primarily concerned with releasing and sustaining the talent of the individual teacher.

3. Supervision techniques should stress warmth, friendliness, leadership as a shared responsibility, full staff involvement in educational planning and teacher solidarity; they should strenuously avoid threat, insecurity and didacticism.

Although subject to modification and criticism, this tradition remains powerfully influential and vital today. It is probably supervision's strongest reflex and most abiding emotional stance.

It is clear that democratic and scientific supervision represent deeply differing views on both the means and the ends of supervision. Historically, as one or the other tradition gained sway, varying degrees of emphasis have been placed on the role of supervision in evaluation and inspection, in curriculum development and in teacher development. It will be useful to describe and appraise each of these traditional functions of supervision, granting that there is overlap among them, and recognizing that supervisors disagree on their priorities and emphases.

SUPERVISION AS INSPECTION

Inspection involves the assessment of teachers for the purposes of (a) maintaining common standards of instruction, and (b) deciding on the retention or promotion of individual teachers. As noted above, inspection was the predominant function of supervisors until 50 years ago and is still emotionally identified with supervision by many teachers. Supervision as inspection is, by and large, strenuously resisted by teachers: when so perceived, it has been referred to as "snoopervision" and "authoritarianism." This reaction reflects the fear and insecurity generated by the threat inherent in any evaluation and "hire—fire" system. However, it seems clear that the community has a right—indeed, a duty—to assess the quality of its teachers and to maintain high standards of teaching. Such assessment is essential in the context of a compulsory school system organized and supported by society for social goals. If educators could agree on the principle that inspection is a requisite of our form of educational system, we might find it easier to handle the problems that arise from its application.

The possible dangers of inspection are real and serious: the stultification of the initiative and creativity of teachers; the imposition of curriculum and teaching policy by fiat, the generation of fear and conformity on the part of teachers, and the like. However, the danger of not developing institutional procedures to maintain teaching quality is even more serious: an inadequate or harmful education for children.

The difficulty lies not so much in the basic purpose of inspection as in the manner in which it is performed. When it becomes arbitrary and productive of fear and servility, it is not simply inspection, it is poor inspection. Many educators find it distasteful to assess their colleagues, and many argue that evaluation is a barrier to communication.

Nonetheless, it is possible to carry out inspection without provoking fear and conformity and without overzealousness.

We do not say this glibly. The maintenance of standards of instruction is an important responsibility which can be exercised in a manner helpful to the teacher. Supervision involves assistance as well as assessment, and should, far more often, emphasize the former. The very complex question which remains—how to assess the competence of teachers—will be examined at length in Chapter Three, but the case for the necessity of assessment must be confronted. We are certainly not ensuring the children's protection by making no assessments of teachers or by making them indirectly and poorly.

SUPERVISION AS TEACHER DEVELOPMENT

Supervision as teacher development focuses on the individual teacher as well, but not with the intent of evaluating him; its purpose is to help him develop as a person and as a teacher. The supervisor tries to define the working environment for the teacher by clarifying the rules, traditions and values of the school; in this role, the supervisor sees himself primarily as a person who helps the teacher to help himself. There is an assumption implicit in this approach that the teacher has the talent, interest and ability to do a good job, and that the supervisor's job is to reduce administrative barriers as well as personal inhibitions, doubts, fears and insecurities.[1] Often the supervisor works in a group setting and tries to establish a warm, friendly, and nonthreatening rapport.

Those who stress this function of supervision reason from several assumptions:

1. That the individual teacher is the key agent of education.

[1]We are talking, in this section, about traditional conceptions of supervision which continue to influence the field. Cremin provides a fascinating account of the Denver program of curriculum revision in the 1920's under Superintendent Jesse Newlon. Cremin sees the Denver program as an outstanding example of public school progressivism, curriculum-making by teachers and national curriculum dissemination. Significantly, Newlon had "a profound faith in the average classroom teacher" (Cremin 1965, pp. 299-303).

2. That given proper support and strength, the teacher's talents can achieve full expression.

3. That this talent is sufficient in the teacher and in the teaching profession to warrant extensive efforts to provide the resources of supervisory assistance.

Teacher development is a legitimate and important function of supervision, since the basis of excellent schools is talented and secure teachers. The teacher needs the concrete resources of books, materials, films and the like in order to do his job, but he needs equally the understanding and support of his colleagues, inner convictions and self-confidence. Supervisors should certainly help to develop these resources, but without abandoning their responsibilities to society and to children. Thus, concern for teacher welfare must, in the final analysis, be subordinated to concern for the children's welfare. Given this *caveat*, we can see the value of helping teachers make full use of their own resources. Extensive research in industry, clinics and schools has revealed a high correlation between the interpersonal relationship of supervisor and supervisee and effective performance. Thus, when a supervisor adopts the point of view that the teacher is the key factor in the education process, he has implicitly acknowledged the significance of his own personal relationship with the teacher. The supervisor must avoid making this relationship a threat or burden rather than a basis for assistance.

SUPERVISION AS CURRICULUM DEVELOPMENT

While the emphasis in both the inspection and teacher development functions of supervision is clearly on individual teachers, curriculum development seems to stress the materials, units and content of instruction. There is, however, considerable overlap in these areas, both explicit and subtle. As Alice Miel has summarized it, "changing the curriculum means changing the people." In brief, when the supervisor serves as a curriculum developer, he organizes curriculum materials, involves teachers in their production and implementation and acts as a resource person for individual teachers. Clearly the development of curriculum is of prime importance to teaching, and virtually all contemporary writers in the field argue that supervision should always include this function. There is a question, however, whether this function can and/or should be performed in such a way as to avoid the observation and assessment of individual teachers. It is noteworthy that the most influential professional organization for supervisors is the Association for Supervision *and* Curriculum Development (italics ours).

CURRENT CONDITIONS AND PROBLEMS

The first part of this chapter has dealt with the traditions within which supervision operates and with persisting controversies over theories, policies and functions. The second part will deal with ways in which supervisors are currently trying to meet their responsibilities.

As we said in Chapter One, supervision as practiced in our public schools has no single, universally-accepted conceptualization or definition. It is possible, however, to make some generalizations about recent and present practices:

1. With the notable exception of many urban school systems, professional educators have purposely deemphasized the assessment or inspection function of supervision.

2. Professional educators generally subscribe to the validity and necessity of a "supervision program."

3. School systems have generally put limited resources into their supervisory programs.

4. By and large, teachers massively resist supervision, are suspicious of it and are reluctant to consider its positive dimensions.

Assuming that this appraisal is relatively accurate, there remains the problem of understanding the contradictory and shallow condition of supervision in the latter half of the twentieth century. Why the ambivalence and the confusion? Why is there not more evidence of dynamic and forceful supervisory programs?

TEACHER QUALITY

Probably the most significant factor in the present condition of supervision is one that is rarely discussed (and almost never candidly)—the quality of teachers. As noted earlier, determining the quality of teachers is a very real problem that is central to supervision. It is, however, a generally accepted but unpublished view that insofar as teaching can be judged, most teachers are not excellent; indeed, most are considered competent or adequate at best. How can it be otherwise when the teaching profession enjoys such comparatively low status and rewards? Repeated studies show that teachers almost invariably score lower on standardized intelligence scales than do other professionals. We know of no public school administrator who believes that he has an essentially brilliant staff, and many who are very much dissatisfied with their staffs. This is not to deny the existence of thousands of talented and creative teachers nor of tens of thousands of dedicated teachers, but the consensus is that teachers in the elementary and secondary schools by and large do not meet their own standards. Ironically, this quality gap seems to impede supervision, rather than giving it greater authority. In one sense, the magnitude of the need for supervision—for teaching teachers how to teach—is so immense that it almost screams "impossible"; on the other hand, there is the anguish supervisors must feel admitting that their colleagues (and by implication, they themselves) are not adequate to the task. The problem of the talent shortage has produced disquieting questions for supervisors: if teachers are so bad, how can we possibly do the job? Or, if they're so good, why do we need supervisors at all?

It may be that a first-rate education for every individual in this country is too ambitious a goal, given current available resources. However, as long as we have made a commitment to it, let us stand behind it and judge our progress by the standard of an excellent education for everyone. It is readily apparent that every American child is not receiving a first-rate education and that, as we said earlier, public education is in trouble, deeply so in the inner city and more subtly so in the suburban school. One factor contributing to this deficiency is the inferior quality of instruction. Of course, the demands we make on teachers may be outrageous and, indeed, many are, especially in terms of the workload. Equally obvious, however, is the need for a much greater number of sensitive and talented people eager to commit themselves to teaching.

TEACHER RESISTANCE

There is another roadblock to clear and vital supervision programs: teacher resistance. The need for supervision—the need to insure that children receive a first-rate education and to assist teachers in providing it—would exist even were there substantially less doubt about the ability of teachers. Theoretically, every professional should expose his work to the scrutiny of his colleagues so that their criticism can stimulate him to improve his performance. This is what teachers demand of their students and what they should demand of themselves. Yet many, if not most, teachers at all levels from kindergarten through ·graduate school (writers of texts on supervision are probably no exception!) are very reluctant to subject their work to professional criticism. Authors, poets, scientists, scholars, actors and researchers are subject to the active interchange of mutual criticism based on the public presentation of their creations. Public examination of teaching, however, is considered an invasion of academic freedom or of the teacher's personal discretion. Why, theoretically, it should be more threatening or unprofessional for a tenured teacher to subject his teaching performance to examination and criticism than for an author to present a piece of writing to a scholarly journal is mystifying, but this view does exist and with great force. Teacher resistance to all forms of supervision derives in part from the historical identification of supervision with inspection and in part from the strength of the counter-tradition of democratic supervision.

The premises of democratic supervision—concern for the individual teacher, full staff involvement in educational planning, shared leadership and the like—have already been discussed in this chapter. While these principles have much to be said for them, their application has been associated historically with a paralysis of rigorous supervision. By rigorous supervision we mean the evaluation of teacher effectiveness and the systematic analysis of classroom teaching. Indeed, the effect of the whole theory has been, in part, to disarm supervisors and gain further independence and security for the teacher. If it is the case that many teachers have a desire to work without having the quality of their work seriously questioned and to maintain their employment without fear of termination, democratic supervision provides the philosophic rationale for such an arrangement. According to its tenets, such an arrangement is not only good for teachers, but also makes for better teaching. The application of this notion, in combination with tenure laws, can make teaching a virtual sinecure.

Tenure laws vary from state to state, but in general they provide permanent employment to teachers after a probationary period (usually three years). Provisions are made for dismissal for reasons of incompetence or improper conduct, but dismissal for the former is rare and can involve costly and extended public hearings. Tenure laws protect outstanding, mediocre and incompetent teachers alike, and represent one of the most frustrating barriers to the improvement of teaching. They exemplify the way in which a response to one set of problems—the protection of teachers from political manipulation—can create a further set of problems.

UNACCREDITED EXPERTISE

There is still another major deterrent to the development of a vigorous and dynamic supervision program in the schools; simply stated, it is the difficulty of determining expertise. Much of Chapter Three is devoted to this issue. There is a shocking dearth of data, principles and technical information —the raw material of a science of teaching—whose mastery would produce genuine experts in pedagogy. Much of what is "known" about teaching (and, by extension, about supervision) is in the realm of wisdom and insight culled from accumulated experiences and intuitions. It is, therefore, difficult for the supervisor to establish an identity as a *bona fide* expert who knows something that teachers do not, and who is therefore uniquely equipped to help the teacher. Teachers are fond of quoting researchers—accurately—on how little we know about what makes for effective teaching and how futile efforts to identify "good" teachers have been. This paucity of scientific expertise lends itself to declarations of professional egalitarianism and individual freedom. It also lends support to the teachers' resistance to assessment. Teachers can cite the rhetoric of science as well as that of democracy to insist that, since there is no "objectively scientific" method of valid assessment, there should be no assessment whatever.

WHO IS A SUPERVISOR?

The questions of what supervision is and should be are obviously very complex, and fraught with conceptual and ideological difficulties. Furthermore, those who expect a precise answer to the question of who actually *does* supervision are also in for a disappointment. It is extremely difficult to find actual existing positions that embody the kinds of functions we have ascribed to supervision. In fact, very little reliable information exists on who supervises and on what supervisors do to fulfill their responsibilities in the school systems of the United States. Few systematic studies have been done on how supervisory practices are conducted. Much of the material that is published about supervisory practice is based on extrapolation from experience and observation. Analysis based on such extrapolation is certainly useful, and probably has a rough degree of significant validity, but it has obvious limitations.

With this extremely large reservation and the related problem of obvious differences in size, organization and traditions of individual school systems, we can proceed to attempt a broad description of supervisory practice. The following roles may be said to involve significant supervisory functions:

1. The Superintendent of Schools is the chief executive officer of the schools and has obvious responsibility for the quality of instruction. As the other burdens of his office have grown, the complexities of instructional expertise have also increased, and the superintendent has tended to delegate this responsibility to an Assistant Superintendent for Curriculum or Instruction, or an Assistant Superintendent for Elementary (or Secondary) Schools. Frequently, this delegation develops into a sizeable office of Instruction and Curriculum with a staff of curriculum coordinators or directors, such as a Director of Mathematics Education or a Director of Physical Education. There might be, as well, a similar office with responsibility for counseling and guidance services. Such divisions tend to emphasize their service functions; i.e., as resources to help and assist teachers and guidance counselors.

2. The School Principal is, of course, the chief executive officer of the individual school and is responsible for the quality of instruction there. The principal's supervisory role has tended to parallel that of the superintendent: he cus-

tomarily delegates this responsibility to an assistant principal or the department chairman. It appears that the evaluation function of supervision tends to be exercised at the individual school level. Clearly, the central office plays a significant part in the process of evaluating teachers; principals and department chairmen participate in assisting teachers. However, the management of schools is apparently so demanding that it typically does not allow school-based supervisors to expend significant energy on improving instruction.

3. State Departments of Education and regional school districts typically make available to schools personnel and materials for the improvement of instruction. This is usually done in an effort both to disseminate good practices and to ensure equality of educational resources within a given region.

4. A number of other agencies also have supervisory responsibilities, though some may dispute their significance in the light of a particular definition of supervision. For example, schools of education employ supervisors for their student teaching programs. Local school boards exert a kind of supervisory influence, particularly in the hiring and firing of personnel and the broad delineation of the curriculum. Less explicit but perhaps more powerful is the influence of textbook authors and editors and curriculum packagers. Although these people remain anonymous to the classroom teacher, they directly and strongly affect instructional practice.

It may be instructive to the reader to know how other contemporary writers see the problem of defining a supervisor:

Ben M. Harris (1963) complains of the limited data on supervisory practice in America and cites one estimate that one percent of the total instructional staff is involved in supervision. However, he goes on to warn that "these figures are a bit misleading, since guidance personnel of various kinds are not included in these figures. Furthermore, titles and job descriptions are so diverse that it is unlikely that all figures [are reported] accurately. Some personnel are reported as supervisors whose responsibilities are largely administrative and managerial" (p. 120). Harris tries to make sense of this situation by suggesting that we reserve the term supervisor "for those whose primary responsibilities are for providing leadership in supervisory activities . . ." (p. 120). The key word here is "primary." To clarify his position, Harris attributes three characteristics to a supervisor:

1. The supervisor does not usually have responsibility for the operation of a production unit of the organization, such as a district or school.
2. He usually has responsibilities in several production units of the organization.
3. He usually has major responsibility within one or more task areas of supervision and has only incidental responsibilities in other task areas (p. 23).

To be more concrete, Harris regards the Director of Curriculum, but not the Principal, as a supervisor. "The elementary coordinator is a supervisor, but the athletic director is a supervisor only if athletics is included among the major instructional goals of the school and if the director does more than coach a team" (p. 23).

Lucio and McNeil (1962) also discuss the difficulty of accurately describing supervisory roles. They designate the positions of "assistant superintendent, director, supervisor, coordinator, and consultant" as the key supervisory personnel in an urban school district. However, they are quick to point out that these positions are "not clear cut as far as titles are concerned; an administrator in one school system may be called a director, and a person doing the same type of work in another school system may be called a supervisor" (p. 25).

They go on to claim that, "It is the extended distribution of supervisory functions among administrators and teachers and the acceptance of administrative functions by supervisors which have led to much of the confusion as to who is a supervisor" (p. 28). It will be recalled that, historically, supervision developed as an adjunct of administration.

J. Minor Gwynn (1961) also notes the rapid expansion of supervisory and administrative responsibilities and the confusion attendant upon it. In an effort to introduce some order to the chaos he comes up with a rather novel (and perhaps desperate) definition: "The term *supervisor* will be used with the connotation that a supervisor in the school is one of the personnel who spends 1/3 or more of his time in working to improve the teaching–learning situation" (p. 33).

Clearly, we are far better served, at least for the present, to discuss *what* supervision is and ought to be rather than trying to ascertain *who is* doing the supervision. In later chapters we describe certain supervisory orientations which have staffing and organizational implications. We are skeptical that many significant or even modest programs exist which embody these orientations.

THE CHALLENGE—THE NEW SUPERVISION

This then is the broad context of supervision: society demands a huge number of highly talented people for its schools but attracts only a fraction; there is a tradition of fear and resistance to the examination and analysis of teaching by colleagues; a relatively sophisticated rationale exists for avoiding the application of traditional supervisory procedures; insufficient teaching expertise coexists with a system of protective tenure laws, highly developed sensitivity to the failure to establish objective methods of teacher assessment and uncertainty about who is doing what in the name and cause of supervision.

We are now experiencing a revival of interest in supervision, and current discussions are refreshing for their relative freedom from sloganeering and pieties. Several forces seem to be behind this renewed interest:

PUBLIC SENSITIVITY

The enormous recent increase in public sensitivity to the importance of education and the quality of pre-college teaching is crucial. The public has, by and large, come to value education (particularly college education) highly, and most people are concerned about their children's chances for college entrance. With the perpetually increasing selectivity practiced by prestige colleges, parents are especially anxious about the ability of elementary and secondary school teachers to "get their children in."

This explosion of interest in college education has been accompanied by savage attacks on the public schools, particularly during the Sputnik era. Although the schools have generally accepted and tried to meet the criticisms of Bestor, Rickover and others, the public is probably not convinced that the schools are doing a high-quality job. And trenchant new criticisms of the schools are being made. Friedenberg, Holt and others find fault with suburban schools; Kozol, Kohl and Schrag portray city schools as halls of darkness. Academic criticism of the public schools is undertaken by Coleman, Newmann and Oliver, Sprinthall and Mosher. Parents, particularly black parents, demand control (and upgrading) of their children's education. Student demands for relevance in their education, which began at the university level five years ago, are now burgeoning in the public school.

This increased public concern is felt by school administrators, who, in turn, have their own doubts. One way to respond to this concern is to develop a powerful supervision program by means of which the schools can institutionalize review, assistance and assessment of instruction.

THE CURRICULUM REVOLUTION

The curriculum revolution has created much ferment, particularly in the sciences and mathematics. "Packaged curricula" such as the Physical Science Study Committee physics course and the Secondary School Mathematics Group program have been adopted by thousands of schools. The demand for black studies curricula which adequately portray the experience and contributions of blacks in this society is a second wave in this curriculum revolution. It is not within the scope of this book to discuss the validity of these revisions, but we should note their effects. The fact that they have been adopted so widely has created the vast problem of retraining teachers in the new curricula. It has also emphasized the dilemma of teacher autonomy: who decides whether or not to teach PSSC? the teacher? the principal? the department? And to what degree can and should the package be modified? The formulators of these curricula are very much concerned with teacher training, despite the efforts of a few to develop "teacher-proof" materials. They are concerned not only that teachers fully understand the new materials but also that they use appropriate teaching techniques.

Curriculum reforms have also spurred many schools and individual teachers to reassess the components of their curriculum. Thus teachers are talking about the developing curriculum, clearly a crucial aspect of supervision. And certainly, once school personnel and curriculum developers have invested resources in new programs, their second thoughts involve measurement of the effectiveness and appropriateness of the new curricula. Hesitant school leaders, of course, hesitate in part because of these issues.

CRITICISM OF THE CURRICULUM

Another important trend in education of special concern to supervisors is renewed interest in the basic curriculum structure. Many people, spurred by the crisis in ghetto education, the college admissions panic and the increasing stresses on children, are engaged in a basic reappraisal of the system of formal education. There is increasing demand for relevance and meaning, particularly from the students themselves. Educational leaders will encounter more frequent challenges to the validity of basic curriculum and demands for alternative patterns.

CHANGES IN THE TEACHING PROFESSION

A third powerful impetus to the increased interest in supervision has been growing concern for the professionalization of teaching. Many regard the professional teacher as free and independent of hierarchy. To others, however, professionalization means insistence on high standards and basic concern for the client (here, the student). Thus there are calls for the policing of these standards by professional colleagues.

Expanded Teacher Roles

Paralleling and partaking of this trend toward professionalization is a growing effort to develop new career patterns for teachers. Typically, and ironically, the ladder to success for a teacher has always been to leave teaching and enter administration, guidance or higher education. School administrators as well as teachers are trying very hard to develop new roles which can combine teaching with other exciting and varied responsibilities. These roles would not only provide for a variety of responsibilities but would also enable administrators to escape the restriction of fixed teachers' salary schedules. Supervisory responsibilities are one viable way of meeting these requirements, and many school systems are developing new roles which combine teaching with the supervision of teachers.

Shortage of Teachers

Still another factor contributing to the upsurge of interest in supervision has been the tremendous demand for and shortage of superior teachers. The huge expansion of our schools, and their inability to obtain and keep a sufficient number of qualified teachers, is a familiar issue. This shortage has led to concern about maintaining at least minimal standards with whatever staff is available, a concern very closely related to the points noted above about increased sensitivity and the need for standards of teaching effectiveness. More recently the shortage has become more specialized, resulting in increased concern for quality rather than a significant quantitative gap.

These then are some of the forces that account for the renewed interest in supervision: almost obsessive public concern for education; growing disenchantment with the basic curriculum; curriculum revisions; attacks on the schools; the movement to professionalize teachers; the search for new career patterns in teaching, and the talent shortage. Each has contributed to a reassessment and, in some cases, to the development of supervisory programs. No doubt there are other factors, possibly including a subtle yet potentially crucial shift among educators toward toughness, rigor and objectivity. (One is reminded of the French adage, "Plus ça change, plus c'est la même chose," and of the tradition of scientific supervision.)

It remains to be seen whether this increased interest will manifest itself in important and valid changes. The challenge for the supervisor is still to meet the conflicting demands of the community, the teachers and the students.

CHAPTER **THREE**

RESEARCH ON TEACHING
AND SUPERVISION

The basic questions in any supervisory conference are three: "What knowledge is of most worth to the learner?" "Who is the effective teacher?" and "What is effective teaching?" If this is the essential agenda of supervision, it is crucial to determine what is, in fact, "known" about these questions, particularly the latter two. (The philosophical issue of what children should be taught will be addressed in the final chapter.) The supervisor must know which of his observations on curriculum and teaching have research support, which are drawn from experience or practice and which are assumptions, value judgments or prejudices about what and how children should be taught. It seems obvious, too, that the supervisor must be familiar with what is known about the effects of supervision. The purpose of this chapter, then, is to summarize current research on teaching and supervision as background against which the reader can better assess the discussion and recommendations concerning methods of supervision to follow in Chapters Five, Six and Seven.

RESEARCH ON TEACHER EFFECTIVENESS

The literature on teacher effectiveness is almost unmanageably extensive. (For useful representative reviews, see Domas and Tiedeman (1950) and Getzels and Jackson (1964).) Yet, *"[after 40 years of research] we do not know how to define, prepare for, or measure teacher competence"* (Biddle 1964, p. 3) (italics ours). No statement in this book has deeper implications for supervision. This situation is explained in part by the extreme complexity of the basic questions dealt with in supervision, the time and research effort involved in accumulating even negative information about these questions, and the fact that no authoritative definitions currently exist of the effective teacher or of effective teaching. However, recent work in this field is moving toward more clarity about how better to formulate both these questions, and some quite significant and provocative research is now going on.

WHAT THE TEACHER IS

The literature on teacher effectiveness is filled with information about what the effective teacher is not and what variables not to study, and with examples of ineffective research. Efforts to identify the effective "teacher personality" are illustrative. With few exceptions, research attempts to correlate measures of the teacher's attitudes or values, adjustment, needs, personality factors or intelligence with ratings of teaching effectiveness have not produced significant results (Getzels and Jackson 1964, pp. 506-82). The same is true for correlations of the teacher's cultural background, socioeconomic status, sex, marital status and the like with ratings of classroom effectiveness (Fattu 1963, pp. 19-27).

In short, "Despite the critical importance of the problem and a half-century of prodigious research effort, very little is known for certain about the nature and measurement of teacher personality or about the relation between teacher personality and teaching effectiveness [or pupil achievement] (Getzels and Jackson 1964, p. 574). Why is this so?

Shortcomings of Research on the Teacher

1. Much of the research which has been conducted has lacked an adequate conceptualization of teacher personality or of its interaction with teaching. Many studies have been founded on little more than "shotgun" empiricism. A hypothetical example may illustrate the shortcomings of dozens of such studies: the Minnesota Multiphasic Personality Inventory is administered to a sample of undergraduate majors in education. Scores on this personality measure are statistically correlated with supervisors' ratings of the subjects' student teaching. Findings, generally nonsignificant or inconclusive, are then reported. What is not offered is any conception (let alone a plausible one) about why or how these measures of static psychological variables in the teacher might be expected to tell us about his effectiveness in the classroom. This is another way of saying that a theory of instruction or, more simply, a conceptual linking of particular personality variables to teaching, is crucially missing in most studies.

2. A recurrent weakness of such research is the lack of validity and reliability in the instruments used to rate teaching (an analogous problem exists with regard to the personality measures employed). These are, typically, checklists which focus on aspects of what the *teacher* does (e.g., knowledge of content, quality of preparation, discipline and control of class, ability to communicate and explain, poise and confidence, relationships with administration and staff, and the like). The rating scales are usually unspecific about the particular effects produced by the teaching and rely on massive inferences by the supervisor. That such ratings are usually based on observation by a supervisor of a fraction of one percent of a teacher's entire teaching compounds the problem of their validity.

3. Further, studies of teacher personality and classroom effectiveness generally involve no control on the subject or content of what is being taught or on the kind (i.e., age, mental ability and sex) of pupil being taught. A personality variable would have to be very significant to show consistent distinctive effects for all content areas and all pupils.

For example, teaching effect (measured, let us say, by subject matter achievement in physics) will vary with the method of teaching used (e.g., a lecture as compared to "indirect" teaching), the mental ability and sex of the student and a variety of class characteristics (e.g., the degree of class cohesiveness or the amount of interpersonal hostility between the students in the particular physics class). What students learn in the classroom is affected by a number of such variables which are unrelated to the teacher's personality. Several implications of this observation merit noting:

In dealing with the issue of teaching effectiveness as a whole, specific subject matter cannot be separated from methodology or from the type of pupil being taught. Both research and supervisory observation become somewhat more manageable (and honest) if the problem is phrased as, "What is effective teaching of these specified social studies ideas to these particular eighth-grade pupils?"

It appears, too, that attempts to study the teacher independently, as the assumed cause of all that happens in the classroom, are unproductive. Research on the teacher, or what he does, as an isolated phenomenon has had little payoff. We are not denying that there are relationships—in theory and in practice—between what the teacher is and what the student learns. Rosenthal's recent research dramatically establishes the effect of teacher expectations or attitude on pupil performance (Rosenthal and Jacobson 1968). However, correlational research has not to date been able to establish as empirical fact or in a causal way *how* this interaction or effect occurs, or how it can be predicted or controlled in teaching.

It also appears that the differences between effective and ineffective instruction are likely to be relatively specific and fine. For example, Flanders (1964) reports that only a twenty percent difference favoring "indirect" as compared to "direct" patterns of teacher verbal behavior had significant consequences for pupil learning. It is unlikely that such fine differences will be registered by the available gross instruments developed for other research purposes. The negative point of the literature is that conventional studies of the personality of the teacher as a means of determining who to select as teachers, how to train prospective teachers or who among them will be effective in the classroom, are largely futile.

NEW THEORETICAL AND RESEARCH APPROACHES

Despite the unsatisfactory results of most research, some present work in this area promises significant ideas and research findings on teaching. Bruner (1966), distinguishing between learning theory and theory of instruction, has suggested the need for the latter and presented some preliminary arguments toward a theory of instruction.[1]

Ryans (1960) found, by statistical analysis, common patterns or norms which differentiate teaching behavior (warm, friendly teaching versus aloof, restricted teaching; businesslike versus unplanned instruction; stimulating, imaginative teaching versus dull, routine teaching). Flanders (1964) has

---

[1]Also see a review of Bruner's *Toward a Theory of Instruction* by David P. Ausubel (1966).

It has been assumed in teacher training that teaching will become scientific (that is, explicit classroom operations which lead to predictable learning outcomes) only as basic psychological research on *learning* proceeds. Bruner's point is that a theory of instruction and knowledge of how to make specific learning happen are equally important. Certainly teaching, as it is typically performed, gives evidence of an overly simple view of the conditions under which an individual learns, i.e., by listening to a teacher talk. (Flanders estimates that two-thirds of all that happens in American classrooms involves a teacher talking to students.) Recent developments in programmed instruction underscore the point that individuals learn in many different ways. More elaborate theory and practices of instruction are necessary in our classrooms. The implications for the conception of teaching as a craft which a master teacher can *tell* an apprentice how to practice seem fairly obvious.

developed a method for analyzing teaching defined as verbal interaction or talk between the teacher and the pupil, and has found that teaching characterized by particular traits (e.g., a high ratio of teacher statements accepting students' feelings, giving praise and clarifying or making use of a student's ideas to teacher statements giving directions or criticism) is significantly related to pupil learning of subject matter. Analogous work done by Arno Bellack (1966), B. O. Smith (1959) and others is opening up entirely new avenues of research on instruction. The data from such studies have been used to test existing ideas, and constitute knowledge from which new hypotheses about teaching are being derived and a theory of instruction might ultimately develop. Some of these category systems are relatively comprehensive and reliable—they abstract the enormous complexity of what happens in classrooms into manageable and plausible terms which allow researchers in different situations to produce comparable data about teaching. Some systems are flexible enough to be modified for quite different research purposes. Flanders' system, for example, has been modified by Amidon (1965) and Hough (1965) for research on teaching, by Blumberg[2] for research on supervision and by Amidon (1965) for research on counseling.

In the area of learning outcome, Bloom *et al.* (1956) have developed a sophisticated way to translate content objectives into specific, measurable pupil "behaviors." The effect of classroom social climate on individual learning is also subject to current research (Walberg and Anderson 1968). All of these studies, and related work, ought to be required reading for supervisors.

THE EFFECTIVE TEACHER: WHAT WE "KNOW"

The effective teacher is not necessarily the one with an honors A.B. (or Ph.D.!), a Graduate Record Examination score in

[2]Arthur Blumberg 1967: personal communication to Richard Weller.

the ninety-fifth percentile, 30 graduate hours in educational psychology, an A in student teaching or an Ivy League All-American record. The effective teacher is the one who responds appropriately to specific factors in the classroom—factors such as the individual learner's intellectual ability, the organization of his knowledge and how he thinks. This is a first-order definition, emphasizing teacher behavior in interaction with specific factors in the classroom. Another definition of effective teaching focuses on its "products" or results. *Effective teaching is the ability to produce agreed-upon educational effects.* It is evident that research (or supervision) employing this definition requires advance agreement on what educational effects the teacher is to produce (in English, for example, the objective of the teaching may be knowledge of anything from *Beowulf* to Joyce or improvement in specific reading skills). Obviously, these effects will and should vary. This is a basic point to which we will return in a moment.

The notion of "ability to produce" as a characteristic of the teacher is implied in this second definition and needs brief elaboration. Having just served as undertakers to psychological variables in relation to teaching effect, are we now being taxidermists? Perhaps the concept of an "independent variable," borrowed from research, will be useful here. Teacher properties, such as intelligence and empathy, are hypothetical psychological constructs. They are assumed to characterize the teacher in a consistent way and to explain his behavior in response to a variety of teaching situations. The trick in research is to avoid already-debunked static personality (or other) variables. The question recurs: What abilities? Let us suggest two such "abilities," at least one of which is a new construct and both of which can be related logically to a conceptualization of teaching.

The first is "cognitive flexibility—rigidity," by which is meant, very simply, the teacher's ability to think on his feet —to adapt teaching objectives, content and instructional method as he teaches to the reactions and learning difficulties of the pupils. As a psychological concept, cognitive flexibility refers to open-mindedness, adaptability, resistance to premature perceptual closure and related characteristics. So defined, cognitive flexibility is hypothesized as one factor—among a number of variables—contributing to the teacher's effect (Sprinthall, Whiteley and Mosher 1966).

A second teacher property which may be hypothesized as characterizing the teacher in a consistent way and explaining his behavior in a variety of teaching situations is the quality of his interpersonal relationships with pupils. It might conceivably be studied as an element in the motivational or attitudinal effect of the teacher on students or in student identification with a teacher and his subject field. Significantly, the interpersonal relationships of teachers and their clients have been studied less than have those of counselors. We expect this attitudinal—emotional correlate of teaching to be highly significant to the effect of formal instruction.

Cognitive factors other than general intelligence have, as noted, been inadequately studied among teachers. Studies of divergent thinking and of authoritarian attitudes are a promising line of inquiry. Knoell (1953), for example, found correlations ranging from $+.28$ to $+.46$ between two (of nine) measures of "ideational fluency" and careful ratings, a year later, of teaching effectiveness. Ideational fluency has been defined by Guilford (1959) as a divergent thinking factor: "the ability to call up many ideas in a situation relatively free from restrictions where the quality of response is unimportant" (p. 382). For example, one of the four-minute tests Knoell used required the subject to "write all the adjectives which could be used to describe a house"; another was to "list all the things that are round or could be called round." The Knoell study is essentially unique in the literature; it should be replicated and elaborated.

The work of Jones (1955) and of Scodel and Mussen (1953) reveals that authoritarian individuals (those with rigid cognitive attitudes) are less sensitive than nonauthoritarians to the personality characteristics of others and to individual differences. McGee (1955), in a carefully conceived and designed study, found a correlation of +.58 between the California F-Scale score, a measure of authoritarianism, and teachers' verbal and overt authoritarian behavior toward pupils in the classroom.

Cognitive flexibility and the quality of the teacher's interpersonal relationships with students might be expected to explain some proportion (perhaps a quarter) of the variation in teachers' effects. They should not be expected, given what has been said before, to account for more or, under any, circumstances of content and pupil, *all* of such variance. It seems likely, in fact, that to the extent that effective teaching is explicable in terms of the characteristics of the teacher, we will find it to be the result of a cluster of what we might now consider unrelated abilities. Effective teaching is the product of many factors.

THE CLASSROOM SOCIAL UNIT AND LEARNING

To further emphasize this point, a brief overview of research on the effects of the classroom social unit on the individual's learning is appropriate. A social influence is unavoidably exerted on the individual's learning by the fact that he is typically taught as a member of a class. How does the class group aid or hinder instruction and learning? Predictably, the research is by no means conclusive. But it appears that there is a relationship between the social climate and mental ability such that particular social climates affect the performance of students of different ability in different ways. Thus students of low ability do better academically in classes which are formal and goal-directed, with little diversity, whereas high-ability students do better in classes perceived as democratic and characterized by less teacher formality and direction. This result is particularly marked with respect to "understanding-type learning" as contrasted to subject-matter achievement. Similarly, it would appear from small-group research that students of high ability learn more in intimate groups than in large classes, while the reverse is true for pupils of low ability. The sex of the student also makes a difference. High-ability girls are more subject to the effect of class intimacy than are boys of the same ability. Other studies of the social effect on learning are provocative. For example, studies by Anderson and Walberg (1968) and Welch (1968) suggest that student satisfaction with a physics class is positively related to gains in physics knowledge but not to measures of science understanding. Similarly, friction between pupils—over either ideas or personalities—was found to be negatively related to physics achievement but positively associated with understanding of science. Again, the essential point is that the effect of teaching depends on the interaction of a number of specific variables—environment, teacher properties, content, instructional method, class characteristics and others—and that the optimal mix is different in the different situations confronting the researcher or the supervisor.

WHAT EFFECTS IS THE TEACHER TO PRODUCE?

We can now return to our original point—that agreement on the educational effects the teacher is to produce must precede evaluation of teachers or of methods of accomplishing the aim of the teaching. It is at this point that the problem moves outside the boundaries of research or empirical observation to confront the profound philosophical issue of what is to be taught and learned. At one level these are curricular and instructional matters, but in a deeper sense they partake of profound value issues involving conflicting social and philosophical positions concerning what knowledge is of most worth. The writers favor giving priority, for research on instruction or supervision, to immediate instructional effects, by which we mean student assimilation of specified subject matter, curriculum objectives or other specific outcomes of instruction. To assess these outcomes adequately is a sufficiently formidable task. Alternatively, "effect" may be defined as the pupils' attitude toward the subject matter, the curriculum or the process of learning. This definition would satisfy the writers as a response to the practical supervisory question, "What knowledge or behavior is the learner to manifest?" We are less immediately concerned, in the context of measuring—or trying, through supervision, to alter—the individual teacher's effectiveness, to establish that the student behaves more rationally or ethically *in life*. Obviously, however, it can be asked whether education is having any genuinely significant effect if it does not produce such changes in behavior. That is why we argue in Chapter Eight that supervision must also provide leadership in the development of substantially new curricula and forms of education. Again, we face the problem of agreeing on the educational effects the teacher is to produce—when, in whom and for how long. The definition of an effective teacher or of effective instructional or educational strategy is obviously going to vary with the answer to that preliminary question.

It seems increasingly clear that immediate educational effects—the learning of subject matter and pupil attitudes toward the teacher, the subject matter and learning—result, in important part, from interaction between what the teacher does and says and what the pupil does and says. While this is not a very profound finding when examined logically, it has taken a surprising amount of time and innumerable studies to achieve.

In making this statement, we are assuming that teaching, as typically practiced, is two things: verbal behavior—talk between teacher and students—and social or interpersonal interaction. (Teaching has been defined in Chapter One; the reader is referred to that discussion.) Teaching, so defined, is one significant variable intervening between the curriculum and the pupils' learning. Teaching is undeniably important to what children learn.[3] This is not to contend that verbal discourse between the teacher and the student is a preemptive definition of teaching or that it is the only way to learn. In specifying the conditions under which individuals learn, instruction by classroom verbal interaction is but one of a number of instructional (to say nothing of *learning*) conditions. In most schools, however, and for most teachers and students, it is likely to be the predominant mode of instruction.

We are suggesting that the "action" in instruction as typically practiced is vested significantly in talk between the teacher and the students. In a very real sense, then, the message is the medium. An important part of what determines the effects or outcomes of teaching is either explicit or implicit in this talk. The research on teacher effectiveness thus seems to suggest that supervisors focus their consideration of teaching on verbal behavior. This position is fundamentally behavioral. It attaches no mystique to what the teacher is or to his relationship with students *in the abstract*. What matters is what the teacher and student talk about, how they talk and their emotional attitudes toward one another.

The problem confronting this approach is that the basic rules for analysis and summation of verbal discourse between teacher and student are still unknown. But, as we noted earlier, research methodologies do exist. Teacher–student interaction can be readily recorded electronically and on videotape. Programmed instruction, in conjunction with Bloom's work, has taught us how to be relatively specific about the content to be communicated. How accurately or validly such content is communicated is a complex but not unmanageable problem.

---

[3]Admittedly, this point can be argued. Carl Rogers, for example, has said, "Teaching, in my estimation, is a vastly over-rated function" (Carl Rogers, Burton Lecture, Harvard Graduate School of Education, April, 1966). Yet, historically, formal instruction has been the essential justification for the school. The writers do not, however, equate education and schooling. For a significant critique of the school and of teaching and a radical reformulation with regard to the objectives of education, see Newmann and Oliver (1967).

Interaction Analysis

Interaction analysis, developed by Flanders, is one of several systems designed to quantify selected aspects of the verbal communication between the teacher and the student. It makes possible the systematic study of spontaneous communication between individuals in the classroom, by identifying seven categories of teacher "talk": 1) accepting student feelings; 2) giving praise; 3) accepting, clarifying or making use of a student's ideas; 4) asking a question; 5) lecturing, giving facts or opinions; 6) giving directions, or 7) giving criticism. Student talk is classified as 8) student response or 9) student initiation. Silence and confusion represent a tenth category. Flanders' instrument, by itself, is content- and subject matter-free—that is, it does not indicate how well a particular topic or concept is taught. The quality of the information being imparted is not recorded by Interaction Analysis, though, of course, it can be recorded separately. What it does measure is teacher verbal influence and the flexibility of the teacher's verbal interaction with children. Flanders' work is also the source of preliminary but interesting evidence on the characteristics of effective discourse between teacher and student. Flanders has found that indirect teaching—characterized by systematic and significant shifts in the pattern of teacher verbal influence as classroom learning activities change over time—is, under certain conditions at least, "effective" teaching.[4] Superior subject-matter achievement was experimentally es-

[4]"Indirect" teaching values relatively more, and makes greater use of, statements by students; integrates student ideas into the content of what is being talked about and does so much more often; asks longer, more extended questions more frequently; praises and encourages student action; makes constructive interpretation of student feelings or attitudes, and systematically shifts these strategies in response to what is happening and to the type of pupil in the classroom. Flanders' work suggests that such teaching is significantly related to how much children learn, their "deportment," their attitude toward learning and their ability to be independent intellectually and personally of the teacher.

tablished for indirect teaching in social studies and mathematics at the junior high school level. Fewer discipline problems were associated with indirect teaching. Significantly higher attitude scores—toward the teacher, the class and the learning activities, as well as greater independence of the teacher—were also found to be associated with indirect patterns of teaching. While Flanders' findings are qualified or contradicted by the extensive research on authoritarian and democratic teaching (see the reviews by Bar Yam (1968) and Stern (1963)), his work is referred to here because it illustrates, and has had seminal effect on, the various schema being developed for classifying teaching as an intellectual and social interaction.

SUMMARY

Teaching is currently defined as communication—that is, talk and personal interaction—between at least two people. To understand the effectiveness of this communication we must look at its content, and at the characteristics of the talk and of the personal interaction.

Research on teaching currently concentrates on this process of verbal and social communication between the teacher and the student. This clearly seems to be what teachers do and what in fact teaching is. It is increasingly clear, too, that we cannot select or train teachers for this process of verbal and personal communication exclusively by Grade Point Averages, Miller Analogies scores, or courses in *Beowulf* (or *Finnegans Wake!*). Using these procedures, we can predict, with reasonable accuracy, a student's ability to complete degree requirements in education and English. The correlation between these indices and an individual's effectiveness as a teacher is, however, inadequately low. Research on the additional factors that make a difference in teaching is now possible.

RESEARCH ON SUPERVISION

Very little research has been done on the supervision of teaching. Harris (1963) reports that from 1953 to 1963 an average of only thirty-six articles a year was listed under "Supervision and Supervisors" in the *Education Index*. Only one article per year was considered "supervision research." And almost none of this work directly addresses the processes of curriculum development and analysis of instruction which we consider the essential functions of supervision. Harris comments: "Notable indeed is the lack of research on the supervisor and supervisory programs and practices in education. We continue to emphasize studies in this field which deal with teacher opinions of supervisors, principals' opinions, contrasting perception of roles and role conflicts. Neither the quality nor the significance of these studies warrants much more replication" (p. 86). It is hard to disagree. Much of this research has been unsystematic and of very limited scope and significance. The methods which such studies typically employ—checklists, mailed questionnaires, recall—are a further serious limitation. Harris' remark explains our decision to review in this section only research dealing with the instructional functions of supervision. Nonetheless, the reader is entitled to a broad classification of the available supervisory research:

1. Questionnaire studies of factors in the selection and training of supervisors.
2. Questionnaire studies of supervisor role perceptions.
3. Evaluation studies of individual supervisory programs.
4. Correlational studies of supervisor ratings and measures of the teacher's personality.
5. Correlational studies of supervisor ratings and measures of the supervisor's personality or experience.
6. Comparisons of ratings by different supervisors.

THE DILEMMA OF "NO SIGNIFICANT DIFFERENCE"

There is, obviously, a point of diminishing return for the reader in negative information about supervision's lack of theory and research. But the inescapable conclusion to be drawn from any review of the literature is that there is virtually no research suggesting that supervision of teaching, however defined or undertaken, makes any difference. Educators as a group can, and typically do, ignore this finding (largely by ignoring supervision). Supervisors should not and cannot. There is a variety of reasons why supervision typically has no measureable effect. A field characterized by Lucio and McNeil (1962) as having "no independent thought of its own," and which can claim only one published research study per year over a decade, is impotent by definition. The difficulties besetting the field are perhaps best illustrated by evidence that supervisors' analyses or evaluations of teaching usually have both low validity and low reliability. "There is plenty of evidence to indicate that different practitioners observing the same teacher teach, or studying data about her, may arrive at very different evaluations of her; this observation is equally true of the evaluation experts [supervisors]; starting with different approaches, and using different data-gathering devices, they, too, arrive at very different evaluations" (Barr et al 1945). One of the writers recalls—somewhat painfully—participating in a carefully-controlled reliability study of supervisory ratings. Five experienced, skilled supervisors did two separate evaluations of each of four student teachers. Ratings were made of eleven aspects of their teaching. The rating scale seemed both sophisticated and simple to complete. All of the experimental classes were tape-recorded and rated independently by an experimenter. Remember the basic conditions: five skilled social studies supervisors, an elegant but straightforward rating scale, careful recording and independent rating of the teaching. The results? The supervisors' disagreement about the teaching they were evaluating ranged from 50 to 100 percent.

Why do analyses of teaching behavior vary so radically? A primary reason, discussed in the first part of this chapter, is the absence of agreement as to the "right" way to teach. A second explanation is the unreliability of the rating instruments used in supervision and in research. A classic discussion of the inconsistency of criterion measures was written over 25 years ago (see articles by Jayne, La Duke and Rostker in the *Journal of Experimental Education* for 1945). A third cause of variation is attributable to supervisors themselves: supervisors either see different teaching behavior when they observe a classroom in action or they evaluate the same behavior differently. Disagreement thus stems from variations in perception or from conflicting definitions of effective teaching. Anxiety can also influence the supervisor's assessment of teaching: "To the spinster, for example, a tall gawky lass who is driving a class either into apathy or distraction by the hesitant dullness of her performance, will be marked up for earnestness and good moral intentions. To the anti-intellectual on the other hand, an intellectually polished teaching performance will be reduced in value by quibbling, denial and distortion" (Anderson and Hunka 1963, p. 82). Supervisors typically see a fraction of one per cent of the teaching of the individuals they evaluate; whether this is an adequate (that is, representative) sample depends on whether one asks the supervisor or the teacher. The fact remains that there are real possibilities for error in the supervisor's analysis of a teacher. This is the problem that characterizes the work of the supervisor and the researcher: the possibility, for the former, of making no difference, and, for the latter, of finding no significant difference.

The point that supervisory analyses or ratings of teaching are not particularly valid or consistent is not made to paralyze supervision, but to emphasize that supervisors must be impeccably honest, intellectually, about their judgments of teachers. More fundamentally, it underscores the critical need for research on both teaching and supervision.

What does the existing research on supervision tell us? Fractionated research speaks in a number of voices. We have already noted that not much of this research deals with the actual process of supervision—or, more particularly, with the analysis of teaching or instructional effect. But, in general, research relating to the process of supervision falls into identifiable categories: studies of what supervisors do; studies of the supervisory conference and its effect; experimental studies of specific supervisory techniques; studies of comprehensive methods of supervision derived from theory, and research based on the direct observation and analysis of supervisory interactions. The rest of this chapter will review and comment on these studies.

STUDIES OF WHAT SUPERVISORS DO

Studies of what supervisors do typically use data acquired from questionnaires or direct observation. Hollister (1950), for example, asked thirty supervisors to enumerate the topics which they discussed with student teachers. Eighteen kinds of issues which were identified were categorized according to the frequency with which they were discussed and the number of supervisors who reported discussing them. The most frequently-discussed topics were professional reading and self-rating. What is astounding, in light of the central emphasis of this book, is that curriculum planning and teaching improvement were discussed by only three of the thirty supervisors. "Social meetings," "etiquette" and "library use" were all accorded more emphasis.

Swineford (1964) studied supervisors' suggestions to student teachers concerning the improvement of their teaching. When supervisors *do* talk about teaching, their recommendations apparently run pretty much as one might expect. In order of decreasing frequency the supervisors in the Swineford study talked about teaching techniques and procedures, discipline and control, development of a classroom personality, planning of units or particular lessons and development of a sound academic background. The low priority given curriculum questions is noteworthy. Other studies have reported the reactions of student teachers to the process of supervision. Beginning teachers have been found to want suggestions (McConnell 1960), constructive criticism of their teaching (Trimmer 1960, 1961), regular conferences (Edmund and Hemink 1958) and freedom to show initiative, and to dislike supervision which is disorganized, rigid or lacking in candor. Roth (1961) and Wright (1965) tried to distinguish between the supervisory activities regarded by beginning teachers as effective and ineffective. Their definitions are so general, however, (e.g., "reviewed the lesson for evaluative purposes") and the criteria so vague ("the effective supervising teacher has faith in himself") that it is difficult to draw many useful conclusions for practice.

A more sophisticated study of what supervisors do has been reported by Blumberg and Amidon (1965), who studied how "teachers perceive the [supervisory] conference, the supervisor's behavior and the apparent consequences." They collected 166 experienced teachers' views of actual and ideal supervisory conferences with principals. Adapting Flanders' categories with reference to teaching, they asked each teacher to classify his supervisor with regard to the frequency of his "direct" behavior—giving information or opinion, directions and criticism—and his "indirect" behavior—accepting feelings and ideas, giving praise or encouragement and asking questions of the teacher. Secondly, the teachers were asked to evaluate their supervisors by the standards of "communicative freedom and supportiveness, learning outcome, amount of supervisory talk and general productivity in the supervisory conference."

The study's conclusions were: 1) When supervision is predominantly indirect (i.e., characterized by the eliciting and acceptance of the teacher's ideas and feelings and by positive reinforcement of the teacher), teachers tend to regard supervisory conferences as more productive. 2) Learning about one's self, both as a teacher and as a person, occurs when the supervisor evidences high indirect *and* high direct behavior. 3) Freedom of communication in a supervisory relationship is curtailed only when the supervisor is highly directive. 4) Teachers were most dissatisfied with supervisors who de-emphasized indirect behavior. The reader will note parallels between the Blumberg and Amidon findings on teachers' views of effective supervision and the discussion of indirect teaching in the first part of this chapter. This study should also be kept in mind in assessing the supervisory methods discussed in Chapters Six and Seven.

STUDIES OF THE SUPERVISORY CONFERENCE

A similar, though less rigorous, study of the *supervisory conference* was undertaken by Kyte (1962). Thirty sets of tape recordings, made up of a lesson observed by a supervisor, a follow-up conference and a subsequent lesson, were collected and carefully analyzed. The teachers involved taught at all elementary grade levels, in most subject areas and in both urban and rural schools. Kyte was interested in the optimal number of items discussed in the supervision conference and in the degree of emphasis which should be given to each. His main conclusions were: 1) No more than four or five topics should be discussed in each conference. 2) The first topic should be used to establish rapport and consequently should be given minor stress. 3) The second and third subjects discussed in the conference should be given major stress. 4) The fourth topic should be given either major or minor stress, depending on the degree of influence desired on the subsequent teaching. 5) The last point introduced into the discussion should be given minor stress and should have a positive effect on the teacher. 6) Repetition, near the end of the conference, of a major point is likely to increase its effect on subsequent teaching. Kyte's findings are by no means conclusive. For example, the assumption that a definite format and ordering of topics is effective for all supervisory conferences seems highly questionable. While it would be a mistake to apply his findings literally, Kyte's study is unique in its attempt to measure the effect of supervision by the criterion of changes in the subsequent teaching.

STUDIES OF SPECIFIC SUPERVISORY TECHNIQUES

Experimental studies of specific supervisory techniques are currently having considerable impact on supervisory practice. These studies are attempts to develop systematic methods of describing and analyzing teaching by the use of information feedback, a concept derived from engineering and the physical sciences. "Feedback" describes the comparison of sample data derived from the results of a process with a specific initial plan or goal of the process, for the purpose of controlling the process itself. The sample is returned, or "fed back," to its source and the error thus revealed determines the kind and amount of change required. In research on supervision, feedback is usually information about an individual's teaching which is offered to him after the fact. This information may be used to determine the degree to which teaching objectives were achieved; alternatively, it may be used as a basis for analyzing incidents or patterns in the interaction between teacher and students. Thus far in our discussion of feedback, we could simply be applying a new label to traditional supervisory practices. But the process has been accelerated and made far more systematic by the development of more comprehensive methods of describing and quantifying teaching (see Flanders, Oscar, etc.). For example, audio- and videotape machines permit a *complete* record of his teaching to be played back to the teacher. The videotape is, in a sense, the ultimate record of teaching and contains much more potential information than does even the most comprehensive category system.

Research on supervision has made feedback available to teachers by employing time-lapse photography (MacGraw 1965), kinescopes (Schueler and Gold 1964), electrical signals indicating student understanding (Belanger 1962), audiotapes (Moser 1965), pupil opinions (Seager 1965), and a number of instruments for categorizing teaching (see, for example, Ishler (1965), Yulo (1967), Brown, Cobban and Waterman (1966), Morrison and Dixon (1964). The volume of published or proposed studies of this type is substantial;[5] we will discuss a representative cross section of it.

"Voices from the back of the classroom" have served as one source of feedback to teachers. Seager (1965) developed a simple instrument on which pupils wrote "improvements desired" at an early point in their instruction by student teachers. This was filled out by the pupils, the student teachers and the supervisors at the beginning and end of six weeks of practice teaching. The changes recommended by the pupils and the supervisors were given to the teachers as feedback. There was significant change in the teaching over the six weeks in the direction of improvement indicated by the students. The pupils' opinions of the teaching were statistically determined to be the factor most influential in these changes. In a related but relatively unique study (Belanger 1962), pupils used electrical signals to indicate when they did not understand what was being taught. The frequency of misunderstanding was recorded and discussed with the teacher in conjunction with the supervisor's own record of the classroom proceedings. Each teacher taught the same lesson twice to different classes. As the study proceeded, the teachers tended to lecture less while general discussion increased.

[5]See, for example, Classroom Interaction Newsletter I (December 1965) for a survey of recent studies in progress on the use of various types of interaction analysis as feedback instruments.

Feedback of this kind reduced the incidence of misunderstanding of lectures in six of the nine classrooms, but did so in only one of nine classrooms when discussion predominated. This suggests that as the method of teaching becomes more complex, the kind of supervisory feedback necessary for "control" of that process becomes much more complex.

The use of audio- and videotapes of teaching as feedback in supervision is becoming very prevalent. Several important research studies have been devoted to this practice. A study at Hunter College, characterized by careful research design and analysis, investigated possible differences in effect on actual teaching behavior among different supervisors and different techniques of supervision (Schueler, Gold and Mitzel 1962). Changes in teaching behavior were measured by the Observation Schedule and Record (OScAR3). The methods of supervision studied were: observation of teaching followed by a conference ("the traditional method of student teaching supervision in which the college supervisor made five separate observations"); kinescopes of the student teacher, directed by the supervisor from the television control room and used as the basis for the supervisory conferences, and a combination of in-class observation by the supervisor plus kinescopes. The study revealed no significant differences in effect among different supervisors or methods of supervision, as measured by changes in teaching behavior. This is not to say that the teaching of the individual student remained constant. *All* of the teachers showed changes "which may be characterized as reflecting improvement in teaching skill." The observed changes in teaching behavior were caused, however, largely by factors in the classroom environment (e.g., the ability of the children) and by the teacher's reaction to that environment ("Two student teachers in the same room with the same supervisor are likely to change in opposite ways."). The importance of studies of classroom climate and of the teacher's intellectual and personal response to the classroom situation (see Chapters Six and Seven) is underscored by this finding. Further, the beginning teacher's teaching was deeply affected by whether he taught in the fall or spring semester. The semester effect contrasts dramatically to the apparent absence of a supervision effect.

When *specific* teacher training objectives are established, videotape has been used with significant results. A supervision study at Stanford University (McDonald, Allen and Orme 1965) focused on the teacher's positive reinforcement of "relevant" pupil responses. Four methods of feedback or supervision were compared; two will be described here: 1) The members of a control group were given general written instructions for viewing videotaped replays of their own teaching alone; 2) The members of another group participated in a complex program of supervision involving videotapes of their teaching, instructions about how to reinforce pupil responses and joint viewing of the videotapes with a supervisor who positively reinforced each desired teacher behavior, pointed out salient pupil cues, made suggestions and indicated effects on pupils. The latter method of supervision—essentially involving training in reinforcement and discrimination by the supervisor—was most effective in producing the teaching behavior specified by the study: the positive reinforcement of children's responses in class. Interestingly and predictably, individual teachers reacted differently to the different feedback techniques.

Various systems for categorizing teaching have also been used as the basis for supervision. Zahn (1965) used Flanders' Interaction Analysis instrument to collect classroom data. The participating teachers were given intensive training in regard to the instrument and how it measures teaching. The teaching of the experimental group changed consistent with the kinds of teaching valued by Flanders. For example, they developed a high ratio of indirect to direct teaching behavior and used praise more frequently to motivate students. It should be noted that other studies (Molchen 1967) using this instrument in supervision have had less clear results.

A general point about feedback and supervision emerges from these studies. Category systems, such as Flanders' or OScAR₃, and videotapes are very important tools for supervision. They make it possible to provide the teacher with selected or exhaustive information about his own teaching. Such information is no more useful or effective, however, than the teacher and supervisor make it. If their analyses and applications to teaching are specific and/or comprehensive, the probability of such information making a difference in subsequent instruction seems to increase. But no technology or feedback system can by itself substitute or compensate for sloppy thinking about the actual teaching.

STUDIES OF METHODS DERIVED FROM THEORY

Studies of comprehensive methods of supervision derived from theory are extremely rare. Mosher's application of counseling theory and method in the supervision of beginning teachers, to be discussed in detail in Chapter Six, is such a study. An analogous study by Bennington (1965) used client-centered counseling as a source of theory and technique. Bennington considered a positive self-concept as the most important variable in teaching success; the supervisor's function is to develop the beginner's self-concept. The principal factor and "technique" in enhancing the teacher's self-concept was the quality of the interpersonal relationship between the supervisor and the teacher. Such social concerns of beginning teachers as acceptance and control were the focus of discussions. The control group's supervisors were limited to observations, interpretations and suggestions about these same concerns. Teacher self-acceptance, measured by Q-sort methodology, was found to be significantly higher among teachers supervised by the client-centered method. Whether this result was related to the beginners' actual teaching or pupil learning was not investigated, however. For the purposes of discussion, this is less pertinent than the general point that, with the exception of the Mosher and Gibbs studies, the literature is devoid of research in which a carefully-developed, comprehensive method of supervision based on theory is applied experimentally and its effects at least partially assessed. One hopes that studies such as these (and the work of Schueler, McDonald, Blumberg, Zahn, Weller, and others) will serve as prototypes for subsequent research. Such a hope is more than pious—the best research on supervision is recent, much of it as yet unpublished.

STUDIES BASED ON OBSERVATION

The stimulus to categorize and quantify what actually happens when a supervisor and teacher confer has its sources in the direct observational research on teaching of Flanders, and the work of Smith, Bellack and others.

The advantages of studying systematically what actually happens in supervision are obvious. Precise, accurate description of supervision is made possible, as are the development and testing of hypotheses about the process itself. The category systems now available are relatively economical in terms of an observer's time and training, they can be completed from audio- or videotapes of supervision and their reliability seems adequate. These systems are very new and subject to ongoing development, and they have had little research application to date. We will briefly describe the two most promising instruments and list others in the chapter bibliography.

Blumberg and Amidon's (1965) study of teachers' perceptions of effective supervision, described earlier, used an instrument to study the supervision conference very similar to Flanders' system for analyzing teaching. Blumberg, like Flanders, assumes that the teacher's learning is directly related to his degree of independence in the conference and proposes that independence varies in relation to the supervisor's use of direct or indirect influences during the conference. Supervision is frequently defined as a special kind of teaching, and the concept of direct—indirect influence is a useful way of examining the similarities of the two processes and of making comparisons with the extensive research on teaching using the Flanders system. The Blumberg system is procedurally simple: supervisor and teacher talk is scored every 3 seconds on the basis of 15 categories ("*Supervisor Behavior* . . . 2. Praise: statements which connote 'good' value judgments. 3. Accepts or uses teacher's ideas: statements that clarify, build on, or develop ideas or suggestions made by the teacher . . . 9. Gives suggestions: supervisor gives new or alternate ways of doing things. 10. Criticism . . . *Teacher Behavior* . . . 12. Gives information, opinions or suggestions. 13. Positive social emotional behavior: statements that convey agreement by choice, release tension, accept feelings" (pp. 1-8)). The principal use of this instrument, to date, has been as a vehicle for feedback and a method of training supervisors in education and industry. The research potential of the instrument is, however, clear.

Other procedures for describing and analyzing supervisory conferences have been developed by Blumberg and Amidon, Brown and Hoffman (1966) and Heidelback (1967). By far the most sophisticated instrument for this purpose, however, was developed by Weller (1969). Called the M.O.S.A.I.C.S. system, it is a modification and elaboration of Bellack's method for the analysis of teaching. M.O.S.A.I.C.S. is a remarkably comprehensive category system which provides objective data about the patterns of communication between the supervisor and teacher, the content of the conference, the logic of the discussion (e.g., definition, explanation, evaluation, justification, opinion, etc.) and procedural aspects of the conference. These characteristics of the supervision are scored from tape recordings of the conference, and the analysis is done by a computer program. While the instrument is so new that it has had virtually no research application, its potential is illustrated by Weller's comparison of two supervisory groups he studied using the M.O.S.A.I.C.S. system—one a sixth-grade team teaching an elementary science study unit, the other an eleventh-grade team teaching remedial chemistry:

> Compared with the elementary supervisor, the high school supervisor speaks more than twice as much . . . teachers in the elementary group make significantly greater contributions to the discussion. The high school group spends 53.9% of the time on methodology and only 19.5% on classroom interactions. The elementary group spends only 27.7% on methodology and 55.5% on classroom interactions. The high school group places the following emphasis on domains of instruction: cognitive domain: 73.1%; affective domain: 2.9%; social disciplinary domain: 12.8%. The elementary group shows a very different distribution of emphasis: cognitive domain: 54.5%; affective domain: 12%; social-disciplinary domain: 28.2%. Discussion of the subject matter *per se* is a significant part of the discourse in the high school group but a minor part in the elementary group . . . In the logical areas discussion in the elementary group is relatively analytical, diagnostic and complex, whereas discussion in the high school group is relatively evaluative, prescriptive and simple (pp. 186-187).

Much more technical and sophisticated analyses of supervision are possible with M.O.S.A.I.C.S.; the preceding suggests how such research instruments can be used. M.O.S.A.I.C.S. is a valid, reliable and relatively practical research instrument which will permit a variety of studies of supervision. While designed to study clinical supervision (see Chapter Five), it may be used with individual or group supervision of any subject, grade level or teaching situation, and has obvious uses in training supervisors. More important, it permits precise and comprehensive description of supervision and, therefore, the generation and testing of hypotheses about that process. M.O.S.A.I.C.S. is the most significant and promising methodological tool so far developed for research on supervision. In view of what it has been necessary to say in this chapter about the research status of supervision, this is a particularly positive and hopeful note on which to conclude.

CHAPTER FOUR

THEORETICAL ISSUES
AND PROFESSIONAL SKILLS

It is essential, before discussing the functions of supervision more fully in subsequent chapters, to identify the broad educational and social responsibilities of supervision in a general and descriptive way, in order to provide a common grammar for communication between the authors, the reader and other writers on supervision. This will enable us to consider professional issues and the skills necessary for effective supervision.

TWO FUNCTIONS OF SUPERVISION

The writers see supervision, generically, as teaching teachers how to teach (which involves working with teachers as people) and professional leadership in reformulating public education—more specifically, its curriculum, its teaching and its forms. These two functions are not, theoretically or in practice, discrete. Indeed, they are coordinate and overlapping. Supervisory programs must be able to perform *both* of these functions and to alternate between them as need be. While we will, for convenience, discuss them separately, we emphasize that they represent a complex web of many kinds of activity.

THE SUPERVISOR AS TEACHER

Our initial conception of supervision is as a special kind of teaching involving a unique set of students (called teachers) and a unique content (called curriculum). A supervisor who functions this way is deliberately trying to educate classroom teachers about the curriculum. In simplest terms, then, a supervisor is a teacher of teachers, concerned with the content, method and effects of classroom teaching. The supervisor must consider the validity of the specific teaching objectives, the problems posed by materials and the depth of the teachers' and students' understanding of the curriculum. The supervisor must decide whether the traditional academic curriculum is a luxury or a necessity for students who do not expect to go to college. He must weigh a language curriculum against one that stresses literature. He must recommend the best from among the multitude of texts, maps and other materials vying for inclusion in the school program.

THE SUPERVISOR AS EDUCATIONAL LEADER

In carrying out these responsibilities, however, the supervisor confronts much broader issues—what should be taught, what should be emphasized, what the children really learn and what materials are most appropriate. The supervisor thus has significant responsibilities for leadership: he is entrusted with helping to establish directions, goals and priorities for the curriculum. It is he who assumes major responsibility for decisions on what should be taught, and who should teach it under what circumstances. Supervisors thus teach, in the sense that they assist, guide and clarify, but they are leaders in that they take responsibility for the direction and performance of others. The word "direction" is crucial: by it we refer to intellectual and professional leadership in the formulation and development of the curriculum. The supervisor, in brief, is the principal curriculum and instructional leader in the school.

We believe it is essential that supervision recognize the distinction between decisions about the components of a given curriculum and issues involving *the validity of the curriculum structure itself*. Currently, most of the energies and efforts of supervision are directed to the former issue. Supervisors and teachers typically ask relatively specific questions about an established area of the curriculum. Should we teach geometry in the junior high schools? Should we stress European or Asian history in the history program? Should we add a linguistics component to the English courses? These are important and complex questions which deserve considerable attention and thought. However, there is also a need to raise questions about the existing curriculum structure and to develop alternative educational patterns. Should we stress academic disciplines in the curriculum? Should we add new courses? Which ones? Does the curriculum need to be reorganized? Are new educational institutions, new contexts and new forms of education necessary?

It is our position that supervisors must exercise a double responsibility for the curriculum: to produce more challenging and valid courses in the existing subject areas, which can be considered leadership in system maintenance, and to revise the basic curriculum structure, or leadership in reformulation of the educational system. It is noteworthy that very little of the literature on supervision deals with the matter of responsibility for basic curriculum leadership. We regard the issue of what is to be taught as real and profound, but believe there is no issue as to which group of school people should assume such leadership responsibility.

THE SUPERVISOR AS SOCIAL LEADER

An extension of this point is the issue of social leadership. Is the teacher an agent of social reconstruction or of stability? To what degree is it the teacher's responsibility to relate his teaching to his vision of man and society? Is the supervisor an agent of the school committee, entrusted with the responsibility of implementing its curriculum? Or is the supervisor himself an educational leader who helps to develop a curriculum out of a philosophic and ideological framework?

Supervisors and teachers constantly face the question of the locus of responsibility for determining the educational needs of the community. Some hold to the legal position that the community, through a delegated lay board, defines these needs and builds a professional staff to administer a relevant educational program. Others maintain that professional educators have a special obligation to help the community define its goals. Chapter Eight deals in more detail with the nature of the curriculum, broadly defined, and its relationship to society. Suffice it to say for now that we believe it to be the professional responsibility of supervisors to confront and contribute to the resolution of these issues. As we have said, the crucial task facing education—and, hence, supervision— is to conceive and develop the full range of conditions under which people can be taught and/or learn. It is obvious that the concepts represented by the terms "curriculum," "formal instruction" and "school" by no means exhaust the range of possible conditions under which learning may occur.

SUPERVISION IN ACTION: GENERAL CONSIDERATIONS

WORKING WITH TEACHERS AS PEOPLE

Teaching is not only verbal communication but also a fundamental social process of interaction between teacher and students. Thus supervision, to be effective, must concern itself with teachers as people. There are at least three sources of problems for the supervisor working with personal–psychological factors in teaching.

The Teacher as an Individual

The first is the teacher himself: his personality, values, classroom manner, his beliefs and their strength, his relationships with children and colleagues, his strengths, weaknesses, sense of humor, view of life, dedication, honesty, capacities, special talents—in a word, the person as he is and as he is developing. Because there are obvious limits to people's ability to "shut off" their selves in the performance of their occupational duties, the supervisor inevitably confronts the person manifesting himself in the teaching role. Some aspects of his personality constitute resources for the teacher and some create problems. For example, a teacher's views on classroom discipline undoubtedly reflect his own experiences with and reactions to authority, both in and out of the classroom. Similarly, if a teacher feels alienated and lonely, his teaching is likely to reflect this state of mind. The effect could be positive: loneliness might lead the teacher to seek a bond with children which could become an essential ingredient in first-rate teaching. A teacher with a naturally friendly and accepting attitude can be helped to channel these attributes to insure excellent responsiveness in the classroom.

The Teacher-Student Relationship

Second, the supervisor analyzes the teacher's relationship with students as people, i.e., his attitudes toward them, his techniques of control, his warmth and affection toward them, his respect for them and the like. These matters deserve special emphasis, because they involve the teacher's ability and willingness to understand and reach his students at a personal level. What is it that the supervisor sees—domineering, authoritarian teaching or simply forceful teaching? Is the teacher permissive or helpless? Are his students affectionate but not respectful? As he makes these observations, the supervisor must also decide to what degree these relationships are significant in particular situations.[1] Recognition of the effects of the teacher's personality on his teaching implies the need for techniques which allow the supervisor to intervene in this domain. Two such methods are developed at length in Chapters Six and Seven.

The Issue of Autonomy

A third problem posed by working with teachers as people is the autonomy of the client, perhaps the most basic issue in the whole area of supervision. All teachers face this issue, but it has special relevance for supervision. It is one of our cherished notions in education that we desperately need talented, autonomous teachers. There are several reasons for this. A first is the belief that, other factors being equal, an autonomous teacher will be most effective. By "autonomous" is suggested a substantial degree of teacher self-direction, self-generation and freedom in the exercise of his responsibilities to his client. Second, autonomy seems an essential ingredient in the concept of the teacher as a professional. Our schools are organized on the assumption that qualified teaching is available for every child and that every teacher is talented and capable. We assume that education should continue to adhere to this standard. It would be interesting to speculate on how schools might be organized if we agreed that we could not find the necessary number of talented teachers. However, in the writing of this book we are continuing to assume that the

[1]What we have said about the teacher as a person applies as well to the supervisor. Knowledge of himself is part of the supervisor's professional equipment, just as is his knowledge of the teacher. It is important, for example, that the supervisor honestly acknowledge how secure he feels about his knowledge of subject matter, curriculum philosophy and his own effectiveness as a teacher; how open he is to disagreement on these matters, and how interpersonally secure he is with teachers. The richer the texture of individual experience, the more one can offer in the way of wisdom, understanding, insight and empathy.

individuals charged with teaching young people require considerable talent and creativity.

It is thus one of the supervisor's major tasks to help in the development of the teacher's professional identity and autonomy; i.e., to help the teacher achieve and maintain an autonomous, individually unique teaching style consistent with the interests of the children. That is effective teaching. This objective parallels a major goal of all teaching—the development of individual skills, attitudes, values and interpretations. The necessity of individualizing instruction and the existence of individual differences among learners are basic to educational thought. There is a basic conflict between the desire of the teacher to stimulate individuality among his students and his desire that they understand his views as an authority.

PROFESSIONAL DILEMMAS

INDIVIDUALITY VERSUS RESPONSIBILITY

This is a crucial problem of teaching and supervision—how to reconcile individual differences and student freedom with the responsibility of the teacher to teach what he considers correct. The teacher must possess some skill, knowledge, insight or interpretation his students are unlikely to have, and as a teacher he has the responsibility of presenting these views with conviction and with the intention of being effective, i.e., of convincing the student to accept, to some degree, his views. (This situation distinguishes the teacher from, for example, the counselor.) However, there is considerable variation in the degree of certainty with which materials can, in fact, be taught. Such conventions as the alphabet, the number system and spelling are not subject to contravention by students. However, such material as the interpretation of historical events and proper usage of language ought to allow for considerable student involvement and interpretation. The commutative and distributive principles in mathematics are not subject to question in the same sense that moral judgments are. There is a continuum of desired student response: at one end are individuality, creativity and freedom; at the other, acceptance and conformity. Teachers must constantly cope with the tension and ambiguity caused by locating the content of the subjects they teach on this continuum. The problem is compounded by uncertainty about the effects of particular teaching techniques for certain curricula and certain kinds of students. In summary, then, the supervisor's concern for teacher autonomy arises from the belief that the autonomous teacher is most effective and from uncertainty as to the "right" view regarding the curriculum or how to teach it.

PROTECTION OF STUDENTS' INTERESTS

In their concern for establishing autonomy in teachers, supervisors also must be aware of the special responsibility they have to their clients' clients—the students. Supervisors also act as advocates of the students to protect them against sterile educational programs and incompetent teachers. Despite the emergence of "student power" and the much-publicized permissiveness at home and at school, students are typically politically weak and at the mercy of the schools. They have a tremendous amount at stake but very little involvement in the school decisions that significantly determine their fates. This is especially true in elementary and secondary education. Supervisors, then, assume part of the responsibility for protecting students by working to ensure them a valid and humane education. However painful the process, however difficult it is to make valid evaluations (Chapter Three documents how genuinely difficult it is), the supervisor cannot escape the task of protecting students from incompetence. To be paralyzed by the complexities and pains of the process cannot be rationalized as flexibility and openness but must be seen as an evasion of a highly anguishing yet necessary responsibility:

assessment. This is the most potentially painful of the supervisor's responsibilities, and the one most likely to create tensions with teachers. It is also the activity most widely identified with supervisors and the one most supervisors would prefer not to undertake. There can be no doubt that attempts to establish a trusting, supportive context are substantially compromised when evaluation (ultimately meaning hiring and firing) is introduced. Evaluation seems to bring fear, suspicion and distrust in its wake. Teachers want help, support, ideas and suggestions but are naturally reluctant to be told what to do, particularly if there is a suggestion of threat underlying such help.

As teachers, supervisors know the difficulties evaluation creates in the teaching process, but as leaders they are convinced of its necessity. The supervisor must concern himself with the teacher's understanding of his content field and the effectiveness of his teaching. Evaluation can help teachers to learn by clarifying and discussing what in the teaching is ineffectual and requires improvement. This implies a further dimension of supervisory responsibility having to do with the maintenance and leadership of two institutions—the school and the teaching profession. In this respect, the supervisor is particularly responsible for determining and evaluating the primary service offered by the school and the profession: the educational program.

Ideally, the supervisor should teach the curriculum and, thereby, a cross section of students. The problem is further complicated by the question of the degree to which supervisors should evaluate within the basic curriculum framework. Is a teacher "good" if he does a good job of teaching something trivial? Is he "good" if he fails to teach something very much worth teaching? At the heart of this aspect of supervision is joint planning of content with the teacher, observation of teaching and rational analysis of instruction. Chapter Five is devoted to a sophisticated method of doing so—clinical supervision.

SUPERVISORY SKILLS

Given the broad educational and social responsibilities we argue for supervision, what skills are required of supervisors? We are reminded of a similar question: what skills does a major league ballplayer need? The answer in baseball lore is that a player must be able to hit, hit with power, field his position and run. A player with all four abilities will probably be a superstar, a player with three will be a star, and a player with two skills may, but probably will not, stay in the major leagues. Our list of criteria for the effective supervisor is, by comparison, more extensive and probably less reducible:

SENSITIVITY

The supervisor must have the skill to sense a teaching problem and its origins. Sometimes a problem can be all too apparent (e.g., discipline or content errors), but the critical skill is the ability to sense a problem before it becomes obvious. The supervisor might perceive that a student's unwillingness to do classwork stemmed from insecurity with the teacher or that aggressiveness toward a teacher derived from a pupil's need to prove himself with his peers. Sensitivity is not to be confused with sympathy or empathy; the kind of sensitivity that supervisors need is professional alertness to the dynamics of teacher and pupil behavior, awareness of what is going on, and intuitional insight into educational problems and their origins.

ANALYTIC SKILLS

The supervisor also needs the ability to make an effective analysis of what he sees—to understand relationships and make distinctions among kinds of behavior related to teaching. Thus he must be able not only to sense problems and their origins but also to trace, dissect, conceptualize and order them in a meaningful way. This ability—to reduce the multiple events of the classroom to a set of inferences or hypotheses which tentatively explains or predicts the teaching and its effects—is one that must be learned.

COMMUNICATION SKILLS

The ability to translate insights so that they can be understood by the teacher is another requirement for the effective supervisor. Obviously, the supervisor must be able to understand the teacher's views and perceptions. To do so is no simple matter. It probably requires common professional experience teaching the curriculum, ability on the supervisor's part to listen and concern for understanding the teacher. This is the same type of understanding needed by a teacher to reach his students and to make himself understood. In the communication of this understanding, as well as in the communication of the supervisor's *own* perceptions and analyses, the critical elements are precision, coherence, appropriate language and level of abstraction. In other words, the supervisor and teacher must be on the same wave length.

CURRICULUM AND TEACHING EXPERTISE

This competence is the hard core of the supervisor's ability. The supervisor must know (in the sense of possessing a great deal of theoretical and practical knowledge) about learning, about children and about teaching techniques. He must be a master of a curriculum area (this could be defined literally as a requirement for training in a subject or curriculum area to the level of the master's degree or beyond) and have in addition a sophisticated concept of curriculum and its rationale, sequence, techniques and materials. A sophisticated concept of curriculum is a *sine qua non* for supervisors. Without it, a supervisor would be like a conductor unable to read music.

INTERPERSONAL SKILLS

Sometimes called human relations skills, this competence involves the quality of the relationship between the supervisor and the teacher. This is the realm of such characteristics as manner, warmth, empathy, authoritarianism, tough-mindedness and the like: qualities that determine how a supervisor relates to teachers as people. Any supervisor ought to have a large repertoire of behaviors and techniques that can be used when appropriate—a much greater and more sophisticated repertoire than the typical supervisor now has. We recognize that supervisors cannot all be Renaissance men. The supervisor is a human being, a person in search of his identify and uniqueness, who as a teacher performs best in his own autonomous, individual style. For him, also, the crucial question is the proper combination of personal and "system" techniques. To be effective with others and at the same time to be oneself is the constant goal of all teachers.

SOCIAL RESPONSIBILITY

The supervisor must, of course, have well-developed notions about the goals of education and their relationship to society. To this degree, a supervisor is a social philosopher, an educational leader with a vision and an educational plan designed to attain that vision. Supervision must involve itself with fundamental questions involving man, nature and society. Without this dimension, a supervisor is more a technocrat than an educational leader. We return to this question at length in the final chapter.

We recognize, in conclusion, that these are rigorous standards. Certainly they are much more demanding than the criteria typically applied in the appointment of supervisors.

In our experience, however, the most fundamental practical dilemma confronting the field of supervision is the issue of legitimacy: how do we establish the legitimacy of efforts at curriculum development, the analysis of teaching, working with teachers as people and reformulating public education? How do supervisors establish their own legitimacy to undertake these efforts? Because we believe these functions to be critical to the survival of American public education, it follows that supervisors cannot assume these basic educational and social responsibilities without a high order of training and of personal and professional qualifications.

CHAPTER FIVE

CLINICAL SUPERVISION: THE ANALYSIS OF TEACHING

A full description and analysis of one supervisory method is the best, and perhaps the only, way to illustrate some specific aspects of supervision. This chapter focuses on clinical supervision, a method which meets the criterion of "best existing practice" and whose controlling ideas and practices are sufficiently specific to illustrate certain of the definitional problems raised in Chapter One. "[It is] probably the most sophisticated and concentrated program of supervision in the country" (Cogan 1961, pp. 12-13).[1]

Clinical supervision was originally developed in the Harvard–Newton Summer Program, a laboratory school operated for the past 15 years by Harvard's Master of Arts in Teaching Program and the Newton, Massachusetts, public school sys-

---

[1] It would be inaccurate to imply that there is a coherent school of clinical supervision. Cogan's brief significant paper is one of the few attempts to articulate the ideas reviewed in this chapter. Robert Goldhammer's recent text, *Clinical Supervision: Special Methods for the Supervision of Teachers* (1969) is the most elaborate statement of the position.

tem. Master teachers, university faculty members and interns join in study and in the instruction of both elementary and secondary pupils who attend the program's summer school. The principal focus of the program is classroom instruction, and interns are given immediate teaching responsibility under the direction of master teachers. Thus clinical supervision is an integral part of induction into teaching. Indeed, it has become a principal clinical tool in pre-service training for classroom instruction. But clinical supervision is by no means limited, in assumption or technique, to inexperienced teachers —it has been used for a number of years with experienced teachers in the Harvard–Lexington and Harvard–Boston programs. Finally, the ideas and practices developed at a relatively advanced level in clinical supervision are quite close to the assumptions and techniques in traditional supervision.

OBJECTIVES OF CLINICAL SUPERVISION

The primary objective—and an adequate general definition—of clinical supervision is the improvement of instruction. In itself, however, this objective does little to clarify what is unique about clinical supervision. Curriculum development projects, National Science Foundation Institutes for teachers and even the janitor who builds a birdhouse for the kindergarten teacher are trying to improve instruction. In clinical supervision, this general objective is translated at the supervisory level into *planning for, observation, analysis and treatment of the teacher's classroom performance.*

Clinical supervision focuses on *what* and *how* teachers teach *as* they teach. The immediate objective is to alter (that is, improve) the materials and method of instruction directly, at the point of the teacher's interaction with students. Such a "treatment," or systematic effort to affect classroom teaching, is not at all abstract in the sense that, for example, a course in plasma physics for high school physics teachers would be. It is this principle of direct application that makes the method of supervision "clinical": it addresses the doing, or practice, dimension of teaching.

A further comment about objectives is in order here. Clearly, the procedures outlined in this chapter can be used to evaluate teachers. As clinical supervision has developed, however, it has tended away from emphasis on evaluation and toward analysis of teaching materials and practices. This is a critical shift, toward the goal of developing *in beginners and in experienced teachers a conviction and a value: that teaching, as an intellectual and social act, is subject to intellectual analysis.* Clinical supervision's adherents believe that the analysis of teaching can be rigorous and systematic, that it should be ongoing, that it requires specific analytical skills and that the professional teacher should be a careful critic of his own practice. In short, the analysis of teaching is a distinct and much more substantial supervisory function than is formal evaluation.

SOME THEORETICAL ASSUMPTIONS OF CLINICAL SUPERVISION

Given the range of beliefs, practices and people contributing to clinical supervision, it is impossible to offer a definitive delineation of its theoretical foundations. There does, however, seem to be common agreement on the principle that *teaching is behavior*—that is, teaching is what the teacher does and what the pupils do, observably and in interaction. Further, when clinical supervisors refer to teaching, they are referring to teacher behavior and student behavior relative to a curriculum and formal instruction in that curriculum. Cogan describes teaching as "the actual [i.e., observable] teaching performance and the results of the teaching." This is as clear-cut a statement as is possible of the position on which clinical supervision is predicated. The emphasis on the results of teaching is important. It suggests that the teaching performance is inseparable from its effects—that the essential point, and measure, of the teacher's performance is what his students learn.

A related further assumption is that teaching, as a complex interaction of the teacher's behavior, the learner's behavior and content and context variables, is *patterned*. What the teacher does and says in teaching content to children does not occur randomly. Rather, it shows recurring and characteristic patterns. A teacher, in communicating with students, may characteristically talk at them, question them or listen to them; intellectually, he may stimulate students or bore them; emotionally, he may be supportive and accessible or critical and remote. Whatever the teacher's characteristics, his performance will consistently reflect some such patterns of behavior and effect, causing teaching (unlike history) to repeat itself.

If teaching is characterized by regularity rather than randomness, it can be classified and studied in the same ways as are other intellectual and social phenomena. The assumption that teaching behavior is organized is obviously essential to any analysis of teaching, whether clinical analysis in supervision or formal research investigation. The teaching must show evidence of consistency or reliability in order that finite categories of observation, analysis or explanation can be used. Clinical supervision also assumes that teaching behavior is, or can be, subject to understanding and control (and, therefore, change) by the teacher. Further, the teacher's behavior *should* be conscious, rational action. Both the children's learning and the teacher's craftsmanship will increase as it becomes more so.

HOW IT IS DONE

The principal method of clinical supervision is an incisive, detailed and complex analysis of the teaching performance whose general aims are objectivity in perception and criticism of the teaching and acceptance of such criticism. What the teacher intends to do, as evidenced in the plans he makes for the lesson, what he actually does in the classroom and the outcome of the teaching (i.e., what the pupils do and learn) are subjected to rational analysis by the supervisor and the teacher. Analysis, in this context, means systematic, disciplined, practical thinking about the wide range of factors which affect the process of formal instruction and its outcomes. Clinical supervision is often undertaken with a number of teachers who jointly plan, observe and analyze the teaching of one or several members of the team. The technique is appropriate, then, to "traditional" teaching and one-to-one supervision, and to team teaching or team supervision within a particular school department.

Whether clinical supervision is done individually or in a group, it tends to evolve in three stages which correspond to "natural" stages in the process of formal instruction: 1) the prior statement (or plan) of objectives, content and pedagogy; 2) the instruction proper, and 3) an after-the-fact analysis of the effect of the teaching. Thus, an ongoing cycle of systematic planning, observation and critical analysis of teaching is the characteristic form of clinical supervision. Indeed, the method is perhaps best known as the P.O.E. (planning, observation and evaluation or analysis) cycle.

The following sections will describe, in a general way, what happens in each phase of the cycle of planning, observation and analysis, using illustrative excerpts from videotapes to give the reader a flavor of the typical content of clinical supervision.

PLANNING THE TEACHING

In clinical supervision, plans are considered and/or jointly developed by the supervisor and the teacher before the actual instruction begins. The feasibility of this approach for the practicing school supervisor is often questioned on the grounds of the availability of time. There is no question, however, that this joint attempt to establish before the fact what materials or pedagogy will work with greatest effect for the particular curriculum, teaching and class of children is an essential part of the analysis. Indeed, it is likely that discussion of these questions at this point is the most effective use of the supervisor's time.

As they plan, the teacher and the supervisor are making "hypotheses" or predictions, based on their experience, about the effects on the students of the subject matter and the alternative methods of teaching under consideration. The plan, seen this way, is thus a set of predictions as to what may or should happen in the class, and the actual teaching is a practical test of these working hypotheses. The idea of the teacher and the supervisor as hypothesis-makers and the notion of a plan for instruction as a set of curricular and pedagogical predictions is quite different from the usual connotation (or substance) of the "lesson plan."

Analysis in clinical supervision tends to be intellectual and rational and to focus heavily on the *content*, the *teaching performance* and the *outcome* of the teaching (as evidenced in *the pupils' behavior and learning*). "Content" signifies the subject matter, the documents and materials used in the teaching and the nature of the problems posed to the class. Analysis of the content usually involves justifying the objectives of teaching the particular content (see pages 84-88); its suitability to the teacher's purposes or to the intellectual ability of the pupils; the teacher's knowledge of and factual correctness in conveying the content; the motivational characteristics of the content, and the organization or planning of the lesson. By "organization" is meant the appropriateness of the planned sequence of classroom events to the teacher's objectives. Planning may be both short-term and long-term. Whether a single lesson or a series of lessons is planned, it is presumed that there is a logic inherent in the content and in how this content is to be communicated. The clarity with which this logic permeates the teacher's thinking and planning will presumably be related to how he teaches and is understood by the students.

Obviously, the organization of the instruction is not entirely separable from the selection of the content and the appropriateness of the problems used by the teacher. For example, a beginning teacher committed to teaching the relation of biological inheritance and variation to the problems of modern societies spent all his instructional time having his pupils solve "magic square" problems using Mendelian laws of genetics: "What will be the offspring of a white curly-haired hamster and a brown straight-haired hamster?" and so forth; he never realized that the pupils were not likely, unaided, to transfer such learnings to the larger area of people and societies.

This kind of careful analysis of the issues involved in what is to be taught and why has several significant implications. Clinical supervision is predicated on specialized, expert knowledge of content and curriculum. The supervisor is, first, a content specialist, because it is not considered feasible to analyze teaching effectiveness independently of the content of what is being taught. This may appear to labor the obvious. Nonetheless, the question of whether people can supervise *across* subject-matter areas is very much an issue in supervision.

In elementary and junior high schools, supervisors and administrators often supervise teachers in several subject-matter areas. This is usually rationalized by the argument that the same general principles or methods of teaching apply whether one is teaching reading, social studies or mathematics. Probably some comments of a helpful, practical nature can be made about methods of classroom management, questioning techniques, how to maintain discipline, and the like which would be applicable in most specialties. Nevertheless, it seems obvious that when a codified body of knowledge or a special skill such as reading is to be taught, the supervisor must know that subject or skill to analyze how accurately and effectively it is taught. Can the reader envisage himself supervising the teaching of German or physics or algebra unless he is knowledgeable about German, physics and algebra?

Clinical supervision has, since its inception, been based on specialized, expert knowledge of the content of instruction. A current and related development, largely attributable to Purpel, is emphasis on supervision as instruction in curriculum. Specialized knowledge of curriculum theory and development is therefore a prerequisite to a comprehensive analysis of teaching. This requirement is explained by the argument that decisions about what knowledge is of most worth affect decisions about content which, in turn, affect and are mediated by teaching which, in part, determines what is learned. In conceptual (or supervisory analysis of) teaching, these variables must be dealt with as interdependent elements in a logical whole. This commitment of clinical supervision to both subject matter and curriculum design and development gives the method uniqueness in conception and in potential for effect.

A Typical Planning Conference

A brief excerpt from an actual planning conference will help to illustrate both the content and the flavor of this phase in the analysis of teaching. The excerpt, while neither exhaustive nor "model," is reasonably representative. Two teachers on the same team, one of whom is to teach the lesson, a supervisor and a student teacher participate in the planning conference. The student teacher is new to the school and to this team. The subject field is social studies for eighth-grade children.

Teacher 1: In this class today are you going to try to stay entirely in the sphere of the 1640's in England or are you going to try to relate it to contemporary problems?

Teacher: I think I want to try and stay with the 1640's.

Supervisor: That's a good point—why? That's worth looking into a bit.

Teacher: Why?

Supervisor: Yes, in terms of the objective of the lesson and so on . . . it seems to me a reasonable question.

Teacher: Well, I don't think—well, to compare it with what's going on today I'd have to use something that the kids knew about. You know, something they were familiar with and in most cases something they were familiar with would be something in the United States. Now—the United States really doesn't have that sort of problem right now.

Supervisor: What is your reaction to that [teacher 1]?

Teacher 1: Well, in my own priorities I'd place contemporary understanding of government over purely historical knowledge, and also I would think in order to understand the 1640's that the students could more readily relate to some sort of power conflict by talking in terms of Nixon versus Congress or something like this.

Teacher: You have a legitimate point—you're right. I don't just want them to learn history for history's sake. I want them to learn history so that they can relate the present back to history, but the conflict that is going on right now—that between Parliament and the king—has been resolved to a great extent in the United States today. There still is a conflict, of course, but it's essentially superficial. It's not the deep-seated thing and it's *not* the revolutionary thing that was going on in the 1640's, so I suppose I could relate it but I don't think it would serve any *really* important purpose at this time and in this particular lesson.

Supervisor: I think, though, what we're really talking about here . . . is the relationship between [the teacher's] techniques and particularly the kinds of questions she's go-

ing to ask these kids and her objectives. Now, if I understand correctly, your objective is to find out how much
these kids have learned about the conflict between Parliament and the king in the 1630's and maybe the early
1640's. I don't know whether you plan to go that far or
not. Well, let me ask you the question: Is this *solely* a
kind of evaluation lesson? You just want to find out if
the background roles that they have studied have taken,
or do you want to go further than that and get them to
do something with the knowledge which they've picked
up about Parliament and the king? Now if it's the latter,
then maybe [teacher 1's] point is worth considering.

TEACHER: It's a combination. I want them to evaluate, and I
want them to use the knowledge to interpret, to go further and to perhaps predict. I'll ask them some predic-
tive questions at the end of the lesson.

SUPERVISOR: Ah, very good. Let's talk about the "going
further." I don't want to monopolize this, but let me just
take the "going further" point. Does the "going further"
—because that's relevant to [teacher 1's] question—mean
you evaluate what they've learned from the roles and
how they can apply this knowledge to the explicit situation of 1630 to 1640 or 1642, or is the "going further"
applying this knowledge to more general kinds of problems about power struggles in government and so on?

TEACHER: Well, honestly, I hadn't thought of that. I thought
of it merely in terms of 1640, but if I do this properly
. . . and they really understand it, then I think they will
be able to apply it even without my saying, specifically,
apply it.

STUDENT TEACHER: Could I ask just exactly from what, be-
sides the role-playing, do you expect them to get their
information? Do you plan to use a textbook or readings
or something else?

TEACHER: No, we're using Educational Services Incorporated materials so we don't have a textbook on this. What they did was they sent us pamphlets and papers. In this case each child received a profile telling who the person they were playing was—you know, how much money he had, his family background, his attitudes, whether he was Puritan or Puritan sympathizer, Anglican—exactly who he was as a person. These are all real people being used in each case. So my idea is to see if they really understood or if they merely absorbed the information and "I'm so and so and so" and then didn't relate it to the rest of the situation.

STUDENT TEACHER: Well, does E.S.I., in the material they give you—do they have any of these more contemporary problems in mind? You know, trying to relate it to "larger" objectives?

TEACHER: Well, that's up to the teacher. I think they should, I think most historians would, as you pointed out, but in this case it's up to the teacher to do as you wish and so this is what I've done.

SUPERVISOR: I do think you might want to make, in your own mind, before you go into this lesson, some sort of decision about, if not exactly how far you're going with this, whether you're going to relate it to the contemporary or more general question or whether or not you're going to stop with the implications for the particular period. It might be wise to have some preconceived notion so that your questions will make sense in terms of that.

TEACHER: Well, it depends on how much time I have—as, you know, with all lessons. If I have time at the end, I'd like to round it off and ask some questions like, "Can you see that kind of conflict in the United States and if so, why, and if not, why not?" And, of course, if I can't perhaps I can do it tomorrow.

Supervisor: So what you're saying is, you're going to start with the application to the specific 1630–1642 situation and if there's time . . .

Teacher: If there's time I'll take it to today.

Supervisor: Does that satisfy you [referring to teacher 1]?

Teacher 1: Yes—uh, also I would presume part of the lesson is designed to develop these skills, as you say on the lesson plan, to "compare and contrast," and that would seem to be a legitimate skill.

Supervisor: Would you want to comment on that? You've really stated one objective as trying to find out how much they know. Do your objectives go further than that?

Teacher: Well, the "compare and contrast" is to see if they don't just know it but if they understand it and if they can use it and if the content can actually be forged into a tool and in that way it would apply to another situation. As I said, if I taught the lesson correctly and they understood exactly what was going on, then they could apply it to situations other than England in 1640.

Teacher 1: Oh, I took that to mean that you were just going to use that as a takeoff point to go on to the Commonwealth period and everything.

Teacher: It's both—as I said—it's both a takeoff point and, on the other hand, it's also a lesson *per se*, an artifact that they can use later on . . .

Joint planning of this kind is, then, the first phase of clinical supervision. As is obvious in the excerpt above, both short- and long-term objectives and the appropriateness of the particular content to be taught tend to be emphasized. The supervisor, as a subject-matter specialist, also raises basic questions about the curriculum rationale. The clinical supervisor's role is by no means, however, exclusively to raise questions. Planning conferences become quite explicit and concrete in their analyses of possible alternative strategies of teaching and in the making and articulating of predictions as to what children will do and learn. Effective planning sessions involve consideration of how the teacher will deal with contingencies, such as a child who has not done essential reading or preparation, and how he will build in alternative ways of teaching through group work, readings, texts, films and the like. The fundamental purpose, again, is to provide a time and a context in which the teacher *thinks* carefully and explicitly about the process of instruction. Teaching is rarely characterized by this kind of prologue. The argument is that there are pitfalls in teaching which can be avoided, that two or more teachers (whether beginner, experienced teacher or specialist in the curriculum and in the analysis of teaching) are better at making predictions than is the solitary teacher operating hurriedly and alone and that more important than any predictions or plans on paper is the continual *process* of combining experience, hard thinking and the making of hypotheses about teaching and learning. Clinical supervision is saying quite explicitly that what happens in the classroom need not be viewed as intuitive or random or idiosyncratic. While, in our present state of knowledge, it cannot be an exact technology, it can be viewed as a series of relatively specific operations leading to hoped-for consequences. If teachers apply themselves to this intellectual task, teaching can become controlled, or at least "systematic," behavior.

OBSERVATION OF THE TEACHING

Most teaching occurs behind closed doors. The historical reasons for this circumstance in elementary and secondary education, and its consequences, are discussed elsewhere in this book. In clinical supervision, however, the teaching performance is regularly observed by the supervisor and by other teachers. Observation is not casual; it has specific purposes.

Teaching thus becomes public rather than private; the professional objective is its study and the modification of its effect. The supervisor's first job, while the actual instruction is going on, is to make a detailed record of what the teacher says and does and what the students say and do. Most supervisors have accomplished this by taking extensive verbatim notes—at times it has seemed that proficiency in shorthand is second only to proficiency in subject matter as a qualification for the clinical supervisor! Audio- and videotapes, however, are increasingly used to record what is said and done during the teaching. Their advantages—a virtually complete sound and visual record of the teaching available to both teacher and supervisor, multiple replay—seem to outweigh their disadvantages—high cost, particularly of videotape equipment, technical difficulties with sound recording, rapid obsolescence and the cumbersomeness of the equipment.

Teachers and supervisors without experience of videotaping often express a great deal of anxiety about the intrusion of the supervisor and electronic gadgetry into classrooms. Their argument usually has two parts: 1) that supervision of any kind is an infringement on the autonomy and instructional style of the teacher, and 2) that the presence of a supervisor and, particularly, of recording equipment has an effect on the teacher and students that invalidates any "data" so collected. Videotaped teaching, it is argued, cannot possibly be representative. It has been found, however, that experience quickly accustoms most classes and most teachers to the equipment. Students do get used to videotaping faster than do their teachers. Technology of this type has proved its usefulness by contributing significantly to the accuracy and validity of the supervisor's observation of teaching. It also permits teachers to see and hear themselves teaching, something which has previously been missing from their pre- and in-service training.

Videotaping, then, is a way to preserve a complete record of the teaching, permitting repeated observation, "stop-action" and "instant replay." It does not in itself, however, provide categories, insights or a conceptual framework for analyzing teaching. At some point, then, while observing the teaching or a replay of it, and preparing for discussion, the supervisor and the teacher confront the question of *what to observe.* This amounts to deciding how to categorize the teaching behavior and how to make inferences about it—in short, how to make sense of the teaching so as to identify the competent teacher or the factors that make for competence and to make accessible the learnings the teacher requires.

A unique feature of clinical supervision is its emphasis on observation of the teacher in interaction with students. The one criterion of teaching whose validity has not been challenged is the learning of the pupils, and clinical supervision, in judging outcome, emphasizes the pupils' responses and behavior as they are being taught. What pupils say and do as they are being taught is the most immediate and valid index of their learning available to the supervisor. By focusing on pupil behavior in relation to the intent of the teacher, the supervisor and the teacher will have a baseline against which to gauge the results of changes in the teacher's performance. Such a focus will serve, too, to keep the supervisor and the teacher from assuming that the teacher is the exclusive cause of all that happens in the classroom.

What pupil behavior, then, is it useful for the supervisor and the teacher to look at and analyze? What pupil behavior is the best index of learning? The teacher's objectives for instruction provide a valuable point of reference. The supervisor knows these objectives from the joint planning conference or plan for instruction. Are the pupils working with or against the teacher? Whether their behavior furthers or impedes the teacher's planned objectives, whether it is neutral or unclassifiable in this respect, is important information. Cogan (1961) suggests a number of other categories of *pupil behavior* which it is useful to observe carefully:

Performance of required work

Performance of self-initiated responses

Problem-solving behavior

Behavior indicating the learning and/or use of concepts, principles, generalizations

Behavior indicating attitudes or changes in attitudes and appreciations

Occasions on which the pupils suggest new problems and new situations related to familiar learnings

Occasions on which they draw conclusions, voice opinions, present or challenge the evidence and the logic of others' conclusions (p. 19).

Once the supervisor and teacher have a clear picture of the range of student reaction, it may be useful to transfer their attention to teacher behavior and other factors related to classroom learning. What teacher behaviors is it productive to observe? The field of supervision is overburdened with checklists and itemizations of teacher behavior. The range of such categories, from "knowledge of subject matter" through "questioning," "relationship with pupils" and "discipline" to "professional conduct," and the like, is probably familiar to most readers. In clinical supervision, by contrast, there is considerable variation in what is observed or categorized, a variation explained by the diagnostic experience and skill of the supervisor. Teaching tends to be classified and discussed in terms of such factors as:

1. *The teacher's ability to communicate.* This involves such factors as the teacher's audibility, the coherence of his presentation, the transitions, the degree of abstraction in his language and the like. We are reminded of a student teacher giving a lesson on currency devaluation to a seventh-grade social studies class. The level of the material might have been suitable to a sophomore tutorial in economics at Yale; the degree of abstraction in terms was such that the children listened uncomprehendingly to what was essentially an excited lecture in a foreign language.

2. *The logic of the teaching strategy or method employed.* This has been discussed above in relation to the organization of teaching.

3. *The teacher's performance of "instrumental tasks."* The teacher may be inefficient in distributing or collecting papers, he may not have extra pencils so that the children can mark key passages in a story, he may talk to the blackboard instead of the class, or have unreadable handwriting or attempt to conduct a group discussion with the desks arranged so rigidly that children must speak to each other's backs. This kind of instrumental behavior, or classroom management, cannot be ignored. The problem can be the opposite, however. Any teacher who has been supervised probably has vivid memories of the turbulence created in him by some supervisor's endless attention to this kind of behavior. The real danger is that the supervisor will overemphasize this dimension of teaching or magnify trivialities.

4. *The motivational effect of the teaching.* As has been noted, the relevance or interest of the proposed subject matter is usually considered at the stage of planning. We refer here to the actual or perceived stimulus value of the teacher's presentation. The supervisor is, admittedly, dealing with intangibles and difficult inferences. Nonetheless, teaching behavior *is* either dull or imaginative and stimulating, and the teacher either does or does not communicate commitment to and intellectual enthusiasm about the content. For example, a supervisor, talking to a teacher about an eighth-grade English class, points out that rapport and motivation were established early in the lesson:

SUPERVISOR: You felt that the beginning of the class set the tone you wanted. And they *were* with you, you know— it was a class of human beings. And kids were smiling and you were laughing and there was just that feeling of togetherness, to use a trite word, at the beginning. Now, the point where you started, "I am going to read you a story today. As we read, I would like you to look for clues as to why this little girl is there and who she is and what sort of place she lives in."

TEACHER: Right.

SUPERVISOR: Well, you did a very good thing there. You put that on the board . . . You took the time to write on the board.

TEACHER: Three things.

SUPERVISOR: Right. "Why is she there?" "Who is she?" "What sort of place does she live in?" Then you explained: "The reason for doing this is that I have left off the ending of the story, and after reading it we are going to talk about it, and I want you to see if you can imagine, for homework, how the story should end." So they had good reason to be attentive during the story, didn't they?

It will be evident in subsequent excerpts from this particular supervisory conference that the supervisor thinks much of this initial motivation was subsequently lost. Obviously, student motivation will vary with the material and with the teacher's treatment of it. To clarify that interaction is part of the clinical supervisor's job.

  5. *The quality of the personal relationship established between the teacher and his pupils.* Carl Rogers has argued that

the quality of interpersonal relationship established between the teacher and the learner has a more significant effect on learning outcome than any other variable. Furthermore, it is probably important to two major kinds of learning. The first is social and psychological learning on the part of students about the kind of society their school is and the kind of individual the teacher is—arbitrary, judgmental, subject-centered, intellectually stimulating, supportive or whatever. Every teacher is, in a very real sense, a psychological educator of children, just as the school has, in addition to its formal curriculum, a hidden curriculum of social and psychological attitudes. Second, there is evidence that the quality of the interpersonal relationship substantially affects learning retention, recall and transfer of the formal curriculum. The supervisor will want to look closely at the feelings the pupils experience, as they are taught, about the teacher as a person. Among the variables which contribute to such feelings as interpersonal anxiety, fear, like or dislike of the teacher are the predictability of his relationships with children, the types of rewards and/or punishments he employs, and his statements about what is right or wrong in children's behavior, in class and out.

6. *Content.* This is an important category of observation. Clinical supervision's method of analyzing content has already been discussed in connection with the planning phase. It is at this point that predictions made in advance of the lesson about the suitability of content, the correctness of its communication, its motivational characteristics, and the like, are studied in terms of actuality. An example from the supervision conference on which we have already eavesdropped may be illustrative:

Teacher: Someone came up after the class, one of the visitors who was observing, and said, "That was a very difficult assignment you gave them." The only way to tell is to see who does the homework. But I was pleased that Ray came up and asked me about it, because last time he just didn't do the homework.

SUPERVISOR: What did you feel about the observation that it was a very difficult assignment?

TEACHER: I don't know . . . I don't think it would have to be. There is a very easy way out. I mean all the kids have to do is say that the little girl is under the spell of a magician. I thought when I gave it that it was an assignment that was as sophisticated as the kids wanted to make it or could make it. It could be just as simple as, you know, the little girl is dreaming, or the student could go into something deeper. I should have brought up things about dreams and about "magic" in the discussion, but I didn't. You know, give them another clue.

SUPERVISOR: Well, you really won't know how difficult this assignment is from the kids' viewpoint until . . .

TEACHER: . . . I get the assignment back tomorrow.

SUPERVISOR: Right. I don't agree with the observation. I had the feeling before you started that it was going to be difficult. I think there are some clues in the lesson that would say that it wasn't that difficult for the kids. [Supervisor presents evidence from children's answers, in class, that the material *per se* is not too complex.]

In summary, then, clinical supervision has both eyes focused on teaching—*in situo* and in process—and on its components: content, pedagogy and the interpersonal effect of the teacher. The supervisor goes where the instructional action is, to record what happens in the teaching and to begin to infer why. While technology can solve the problem of selective, biased perception by recording the exact process of instruction, the hard thinking about that enormously complex process remains to be done.

EVALUATION OR ANALYSIS AFTER THE TEACHING

The crucial phase in the analysis of instruction is the conference following the teaching. If the conference occurs immediately after the teaching, the perceptions and feelings of both supervisor and teacher are still fresh and acute. There can be disadvantages to an immediate conference, however. Feelings may be *too* acute (the teacher may be discouraged or defensive or "unobjective"). Further, the supervisor is at a distinct disadvantage if he does not have enough time to review the data derived from observation and to begin the process of making tentative inferences and deciding what the data appear to say about the content, the method of teaching and what the children are learning. He needs time, too, to decide upon a plan or agenda for the supervision session. Sufficient time, then, for the supervisor and teacher to think, and for the teacher to catch his breath emotionally, is very important to the outcome of the conference itself.

Identifying Recurrent Patterns in the Teaching

Analysis of the teaching performance can be conducted on several levels, the most complex of which concern abstractions or numerous variables. Let us consider first the types of analysis which are usually rejected in clinical supervision:

The most common of these is the simple *inventory*, or list, of the events of the teaching period. A series of discrete events in the teaching is noted and assigned cause-and-effect relationships by the supervisor. These are recapitulated for the teacher, correlated and checked off as "covered." Such supervision is descriptive, *ad hoc* and unanalytic. A second kind of analysis focuses on *critical incidents*. Details are played down, and the supervisor tends to deal principally with what he sees as turning points or critical events in the teaching. This is rather like reading a novel for lurid passages of violence or sex. The result may be a stimulating hour, but one's understanding of the plot, characterization and "meaning" will be distorted. The problem with this approach is that critical incidents are analyzed without trying to help the teacher understand why they became critical or to see them as something more than separate incidents, in the most literal sense of both words. The kind of reading and thought which goes into textual analysis is a better analogy for the level of analysis aimed for in clinical supervision.

The most complex and valuable level of supervisory analysis involves identifying *recurrent patterns* in what is being taught, in the teaching itself and in the ways students respond. When these patterns are brought to the attention of the teacher, in connection with alternatives available to him, they may help him to change his teaching behavior. It should be remembered that the analysis of teaching is a means to *change* teaching behavior, that is, to encourage teachers to behave in particular ways as they teach. This is what is meant in clinical supervision by the objective of "the improvement of instruction." In clinical supervision an attempt is made to direct the post-teaching conference toward discussion of *recurring patterns* in content, teaching or student behavior and of their *possible interrelations*. We have already noted the assumption in clinical supervision that teaching is organized or patterned behavior. Cogan provides a useful example of such a pattern, and discusses its implications:

A student teacher was attempting to have his class arrive at some critically examined generalizations about the characteristics of American heroes. A portion of the discussion went as follows:

Pupil: Jesse James stole from the rich to give to the poor.

Teacher: Since a robber obviously can be a hero, we had better cross "honesty" off our list of characteristics.

Second Pupil: Our heroes come from the common people like Abraham Lincoln.

Teacher: So we can say that one characteristic of the American hero is humble origin.

THIRD PUPIL: Billy the Kid . . .

TEACHER: (interrupts) Yes, a great gunfighter.

FOURTH PUPIL: Andrew Jackson was a great fighter too. He came from the common people and fought for their rights.

TEACHER: Look on page 237 in your text and you will find proof of that. Now we've had characteristics of common origin, love of common people, personal bravery, and so on. Now Andrew Jackson . . .

Such interchanges took place several times in the course of the lesson. The period had started well, but had ended in inattention and disorder. What is the pattern? The pupils propose an idea, the teacher elaborates it. The pupils make single contributions, the teacher makes the generalization. The pupils make assertions, the teacher finds evidence for them. The meaning of the pattern? It may be that the teacher sees himself as *the* active person in the classroom transactions. He casts the pupils in the role of suppliers of facts and single ideas. He himself evaluates, elaborates, proves, and draws conclusions.

This is not a great and dramatic insight, but it does help to make sense for the student teacher of what before seemed to be unconnected events. It permits him to make an informed guess as to why the class became disorderly at the end of the period. But more important, the teacher has seen his own behavior and can be helped directly in planning to improve (1) his perception of what the teacher should do, and (2) how to teach from within the implications of this perception" (pp. 27-28).

A further example of the analysis of teaching patterns and alternative approaches may be useful to the reader. A teacher has read a short story, "The Little Girl of the Sea," to an eighth-grade English class. The children follow attentively and with apparent interest. The teacher then proceeds to question them for their interpretations of the story. His questioning is hurried, rhetorical and makes little intellectual demand on the students. The effect of the questions is to put the teacher's answers in the children's mouths. The students do not cause the teacher trouble; rather, they become confused and passive. The following discussion between the supervisor and the teacher occurs about halfway through the supervisory conference:

SUPERVISOR: Let's talk about the way the class responded, as compared to how you might have wanted them to respond. The first question you asked when you finished reading was, "What's the thing that you know most about the little girl?" At that point, six hands went up. You took one response. After you took the response, you moved immediately to the next question. You made a choice there, consciously or unconsciously: "I am not going to take six responses, I'm going to take one response." O.K. Think what's happening in your mind, as compared to what's happening in their minds. Then you said, "Is there something else we know about the little girl?" This question seemed to say to me, "The first response I got is a nice response, but it isn't what I want. Is there something else we know about the little girl?" No hands were up; you got no response. Then you said, "Well, what's strange about the little girl?" One hand went up, one response. Then you asked, "Does she miss people?" No hands went up. Then you said, "Well, look on page 2," and you read the passage, and then you rephrased the same question. One hand went up; you took the response. You said, "Right." Then you gave a statement of conclusion, what that answer meant. Then you asked, "What sort of sentence is that?" You had no hands up; you got no response. You gave the answer to the question. Then you said, "Can you think of anything else?" One hand went up; you took one response. You said, "Right." Then you gave a concluding sentence, what that answer meant. Then this is the point where you felt you had to draw a conclusion from this sequence of questions and responses, and you said, "These are the two important things about the girl," and you wrote them on the board. "She's lonely and she is . . ." whatever the second was.

TEACHER: Ageless.

SUPERVISOR: "Ageless." Well, let's stop at that point. You know, is there anything in that pattern of questioning or that sequence of questioning that gives you any clues to the way the class was responding or not responding and why?

TEACHER: Well, let me answer sort of a different question and see if that won't work it out. I think that this was a mistake. And I have noticed that while I'm looking for class participation, I'm looking for what *I* want from them. In other words, I'm not really trying to get class participation. I could have asked a question that could have gotten all six people talking, who raised their hands at first, which might have brought about other things without me having to aim for them. Because I got my answer, I put it on the board, and went on to the next. Then the kids say to themselves, "Oh-oh, he wants a special answer. I'd better be very careful with what I say or I'm not going to get the right answer." In other words, they would be more worried about whether they gave the right answer rather than just participating in some little discussion of what's going on in the story. In other words, I turned the kids away from the story to me and I kept on manipulating the classroom for my answers rather than trying to find out what they thought. And in a certain way I could defend that, by saying that this might have been necessary for them to understand the story, but I think that they could have done better and I think that possibly they would understand more if I hadn't.

SUPERVISOR: Is there another hypothesis here that we haven't examined? You think this was necessary for them to understand the story. With the exception of the first question, each time you asked a question, you got a response. Then the hypothesis is, "I got the answer, they are moving with me."

TEACHER: Yeah, when the fact was that I got the answer I wanted. I just assumed that they were with me.

SUPERVISOR: Because there is a lesson up there in your mind, you know. It's clicking along piece by piece.

TEACHER: Exactly. In fairness to me I think I did try to check out some other kids. Like when I called on Wayne in the back of the room and asked him. You know, sometimes I sort of harped on things, it seemed to me, from different people. But you're right.

SUPERVISOR: But I think your observation about the things they were picking up after that first questioning sequence—you know, what clues were the kids picking up, consciously or unconsciously—is a very important one. I mean your observation about "Mr. Jones is looking for an answer and he will ask a question till he gets that answer, and then he is going to give the meaning of the answer." You did do that every time, it's true. Here is the answer, this is what it means, and you gave a little statement of conclusion and moved on to the next question.

TEACHER: Exactly. That goes back to playing God in the classroom, which was what I was trying to get away from. Yeah, I don't think that was very good.

SUPERVISOR: What are the alternatives?

TEACHER: Well, this is the difficulty. It's really hard for me to work out an alternative now. I will have to think about that. I can't really answer that now.

SUPERVISOR: One base for working out an alternative, you know, is to think in terms of an analogy that I like to use: this is my lesson up here in my head that is making these turns one cog at a time. What assurance can I build into the thing that the class—22 people—is going to move that way also?

TEACHER: Right. The question is whether you're going to put the emphasis on the kids or on the lesson, and I put the emphasis on the lesson.

SUPERVISOR: Sometimes, in some settings, that amounts to deciding at a given point in the lesson that you want the focus to lead to a conclusion. So you break the class up into little groups and let them try to get to that conclusion. Then you talk about, "What conclusion did you come to, what conclusion did *you* come to, what conclusion did *you* come to?" and that gives the clue to the kids that it's important that they come to the conclusion. The clues they were picking up from this sequence were, "He knows what questions he wants answered, and then he will tell us the significance of the answer when he gets the answer." So at that point in my mind the kids can tune out. I don't mean turn off, I mean tune out of the activity. They can go back into neutral. You had them in gear and they were moving along nicely and then you put them in neutral again with that questioning sequence.

TEACHER: Right . . .

SUPERVISOR: May I make a further suggestion along this line? And that is that instead of asking a question of fact like, "Where is she?" you can ask the question that forces them to use that fact: "What do you make of where she is?" Assume they can't answer that question. Then you ask, "Well, where is she?" Then back, "What do you make of that?" In other words, if you ask them a big question and they can't answer it, then you can always ask the factual question. Another example is, "What do you make of the difference between her town and our town?" This is level two. Level one is, "What are the differences between her town and our town?" Then the next question is, "What do you make of that?" You can turn those upside down and say, "What do you make of the differences between her town and our town?" And then there is no response. "Well, what *are* the differences between her town and our town?"

TEACHER: My problem here is that I've had a great deal of difficulty getting simple answers.

SUPERVISOR: Well, that's what I mean. I don't say to you, Get the simple answers. I'm hypothesizing that you can't get the simple answers and you can maybe give them a question that engages their minds more.

TEACHER: Oh, I see.

SUPERVISOR: A simple question may be not challenging them to think, because it's an obvious answer or they feel the answer is easy so they don't go looking for it. They're not motivated enough to seek the answer. Another example might be, "What do the details of the picture tell you?" Or, rather, "If you saw the photographs she found of the woman and the man, what would you make of it?" No response. "Well, how was the man dressed in the photograph?" And then another example, "The story tells you where she is. What do you make of that?" Not "Where is she? What do you make of it?" as two questions, but as one question which forces them to use facts to construct hypotheses to use their imaginations. In other words, this seems to me to be in line with what you want to do or what you want them to do.

TEACHER: That's good.

SUPERVISOR: Or another example, "How can you explain that no ships see her village? How can you explain that the boat goes right over her? How do you explain that?" Instead of asking for the facts and then coming to the conclusion. I think this is very important because the effect of doing this is the effect of building a problem context. So the kids perceive the problem context: "Here's a problem to solve," and then you ask the factual question that will help them solve the problem. "How do you explain . . ." "Well then, what is . . ." Then they have a context for the "What is" question. It leads to the solution of that particular problem.

TEACHER: That's good, that's good.

This excerpt merits a brief commentary. It is interesting to note the supervisor's extensive use of evidence. He draws on detailed notes in his first remarks to the teacher. Indeed, he has almost a complete text of what happened in class. With the teacher he identifies the central pattern and "problem" in the teaching. In a summary not included in the excerpt he puts the problem directly:

SUPERVISOR: You know, I thought you had 22 kids with you, and I really had the feeling that they were there with you; there was no barrier between you at all, no screen, no wall. All working together. Then you started the reading, you started the questioning sequence, and gradually the kids went into neutral or you disengaged them, and my hypothesis is that this happened because of the questioning pattern, their response pattern, and your giving conclusions to responses and doing all the work. The problem as I see it is to maintain the engagement; you know, if you really want the class to focus on a conclusion or lead to a conclusion or lead to an understanding, then somehow you have to devise the means to let them do that work instead of your doing it.

The supervisor then raises the question of how, pedagogically, to avoid "disengaging" the students, and proceeds to teach the teacher two methods: the use of small groups and two in-

terrelated questioning procedures which effectively let the
pupils do the intellectual work. The supervisor is direct, businesslike and relatively didactic. Yet the teacher plays a significant intellectual part in the analysis of what went wrong.

Reinforcing Successful Teaching
The fourth and most comprehensive supervisory strategy is,
then, to identify the most prominent behaviors and patterns
of instruction, select those that can be changed and offer suggestions for the development of more effective teaching.
Change is built on successful elements in the teaching performance and on the teacher's own abilities, preferences and
views of what a competent teacher does. Thus, successful elements in the teaching must be rewarded with praise. What
has worked for the teacher can be one of the most useful
models for him to follow. Reinforcement has the additional
effect of allaying somewhat the teacher's anxiety about the
analysis of his teaching. Such anxiety is *always* present, for
the beginner and the experienced teacher. He has understandable fears that his teaching will be found wanting or that he,
not his teaching, is being evaluated.

The conclusion of the supervisory conference from which
we just quoted illustrates the reinforcement of successful elements in the teaching:

SUPERVISOR: I'd like to leave it perfectly clear in your mind
that I think, from what I see—the way I see you working
and the way I've seen others work—that I would predict
that you will have a very high degree of success in working with young people. The reason I say this is that
there is incontrovertible evidence that you are really
thinking of them and thinking of their problems, and I
would just like to recite my evidence for that conclusion. Some of this may seem very small, but to me it is
very significant. First, you knew their names; you knew
their names when you started. How many teachers know

the kids' names? How many teachers *care* about the names? Your knowing their names said to them incontrovertibly, "He wants to know me, he cares about me as an individual. I matter." Then another thing—you mentioned writing on the board, which is simply considerate of them, but the thing that lit up for me was, "Do you have any questions before we begin reading?" I think this is a very, very important and good thing to do, because instead of keeping everybody off balance, you keep putting the kids on balance, you see. Instead of knocking them about with your questions or with your assignments or with your procedures, you're constantly getting them set in balance. You put it on the board so that they can read it, you ask them if there are any questions before you begin; there aren't any. Another piece of evidence is your reading . . . I say *do* read to kids because you read beautifully, and it's an important part of their education, too, to hear literature—not hyperdramatic, but just good, solid, straight reading like Frost read his stuff. You read that way—straight and powerfully.

It hardly needs remarking that the teacher, hearing these comments, is likely not only to feel good, and encouraged professionally, but also to repeat these particular teaching behaviors.

Two general points should be made here. Clinical supervision aims to help the teacher capitalize on his strengths, compensate for his weaknesses and develop his own individual and "best" teaching style. The means of doing so, derived from reinforcement theory in learning, is to reinforce effective teaching and permit ineffective teaching to extinguish. Second, within the very broad limits of competence defined by the supervisor, the teacher has freedom and is urged to develop a teaching style of his own. The autonomy of the teacher, is, then, both a strategy and a belief about the individual and learning. The current research, reviewed in Chapter Three, does not justify a single view of effective teaching or the effective teacher. The individual's teaching is probably an expression of long-established behavior patterns, and is most authentic and effective when it is a developed, disciplined personal expression, rather than an imitative or derivative behavior. The clinical supervisor thus forms hypotheses about appropriate change in the teaching while continuing to value the teacher's personal and professional autonomy. "Personality factors," in particular are outside the jurisdiction of the clinical supervisor. "[The] purposes [of clinical supervision] are to improve teaching performance, not to reform personality; the proper subject of supervisory sessions is [teaching] behavior, not persons; and the major goal is constructive, not merely critical" (Cogan 1961, p. 14).

Some pragmatic "tricks of the trade" have been found productive in this post-teaching analysis session. The supervisor should plan a strategy for each conference, as well as a long-range supervisory program for each teacher. Time invested in studying the data or videotape of the teaching performance, and in making inferences about it, pays off. A limited number —two or three, as a rule of thumb—major points or interpretations of what is happening in, or affecting, the teaching may be the most productive kind of agenda. "The honest, tough, objective facts of the performance" (p. 29) should be the basic material of the analysis. Reinforcement of the effective elements in the teaching is crucial. One student teacher described the alternative approach quite succinctly: "My supervisor is very specific about the things in my teaching which are ineffective and very infrequent in commenting on anything which I do well." The supervisor should also avoid making "moral" or value judgments about the teaching or the teacher ("Your handling of the commutative principle was particularly *good*," or "The group work went *badly*, I thought.") It is important to avoid the implication that teaching behavior is "good" or "bad" rather than functional or appropriate to particular content and learning objectives. This principle is consistent with the already-noted shift in clinical supervision from evaluation (Is this teacher certifiable? Should he receive tenure?) to analysis of curriculum issues and instructional practices. It is consistent, too, with a view of supervision as an *instructional process*, focusing on the development of curriculum and the analysis of teaching, rather than as personnel evaluation.

A common format for the group analysis session has the teacher begin by discussing his perceptions of what happened in the lesson and why. The supervisor may want the teacher to probe some of these perceptions in depth. The supervisor then calls for analysis from other teachers who have observed the teaching. These several views of what happened and why and what this implies for the subsequent instruction are considered carefully by the group. The next lesson is then planned on the basis of this pooled analysis. Variations on this format occur, of course, but it has been found to be productive. Eventually the group reaches a certain measure of agreement (and disagreement) as a result of careful analyses, the thorough airing of perceptions and interpretations, increasing group familiarity with and observation of the individual's teaching, increasing skill in analysis or, on occasion, fatigue or accession to the supervisor. When this stability has been achieved, the emphasis shifts to consequences, and to planning for the next teaching session. This is as it should be: planning should develop from and supersede analysis; it is the main purpose of the analysis. It is in the planning stage that insights from the foregoing analysis must be put (and made) to work. Unless the teaching, and the children's learning, is modified—improved—there is little, if any, point to the analysis session.

SUMMARY AND IMPLICATIONS

We have described and illustrated at considerable length how the clinical supervisor works, in an attempt to make a method of supervision explicit. A single chapter cannot be more, however, than a conceptual statement. It should be stressed that we have *not defined*, but only characterized, a wide range of supervisory practice. What began more than a decade ago as a way to train beginning teachers—the vicarious involvement of the student teacher in the teaching act by its analysis—has become a much more comprehensive set of objectives, assumptions and procedures for training and involving both beginning and experienced teachers with the content and the practice of teaching.

The basic method of clinical supervision is systematic rational study and analysis of teaching. Its aim is to induce teachers to think about and then implement new ways of teaching. The methodology is didactic: reinforcement of effective teaching, analysis leading to rational understanding or insight, instruction in new curricula and methods of teaching and observation of the teaching of others.

Clinical supervision is a practical way to modify the deficiencies of formal curriculum and instruction and of the institution, the school, in which instruction is undertaken. The protection of the client—that is, the pupil—and the upgrading of the occupation of teaching require some kind of "quality control" of curriculum, subject matter content and teaching. Supervision defined as quality control is a *conservative* function. Its effect is to ensure or "guarantee" that the existing curriculum and subject disciplines are validly taught. Defined more broadly, clinical supervision also addresses itself to the enormous ongoing problem of curriculum *development* and the improvement of instruction which confronts American education. To solve these problems requires radical and continuing change. Clinical supervision is one means by which teachers can confront and modify both the content and the practice of teaching. Indeed, it is virtually inseparable from curriculum development activity, both in its theoretical principles and as a strategy for involving teachers in analysis of their instruction. The most productive way to get teachers to analyze and change *how* they teach, in the writer's experience, is to involve them in analysis of *what* they teach. In regard to quality control, clinical supervision is clearly anchored in specialization in subject matter.

Clinical supervision is vulnerable, in part because it chooses to concern itself with the practice of instruction, a form of behavior which is exceedingly complex and imperfectly understood. In addition, the supervisor faces at least two very real institutional risks, from the right and the left. Teachers are ready to cry "impractical" or "foul" over invasion of their autonomy, while academics tend to decry any concern with pedagogy, particularly among their colleagues in education. Educational researchers say "too soon," or insist that "we do not know how to define, prepare for or measure teacher competence."

Clinical supervision is full of gaps. It is a fact—an extremely sobering one—that we don't know, either theoretically or empirically, who the effective teacher is or what effective teaching is. It is a fact that there is evidence of very low validity and reliability in the analyses, inferences and evaluations supervisors make about teaching behavior. It is a fact that there is no conclusive empirical evidence that clinical supervision changes what teachers do. We do, however, have significant clinical opinion and experience on these questions. A decade of practice, some attempt to conceptualize clinical supervision and considerable experience suggest that this method of instructing teachers *does* make a difference.

The case for clinical supervision rests, in the final analysis, on a set of beliefs concerning how we acquire knowledge about, and how we can change, complex educational phenomena. A first premise is that what and how children are taught in schools, *now*, does matter. Greater understanding and control of these processes cannot wait upon (and indeed may never be achieved by) "pure" research in the sciences basic to teaching: psychology, learning theory and sociology. The clinical supervisor is thus, in a sense, symbolic. He represents training and intelligence applied to the means by which children are taught. His is a commitment to hard thinking about processes affecting millions of children. It is reasonable to expect from his work the development of a high order of clinical judgment, that is, experience-based learning or wisdom concerning problematic curriculum and instructional issues. Still, understanding of the complicated intellectual and social act of teaching will require an application of much more intelligence at all levels—theory, research and applied analysis—than has so far been expended. Ultimately, clinical supervision attests to a belief that intelligence and rational analysis applied to a problem, even one as complicated and slippery as the craft of teaching, will pay off. That, if nothing else about the method, seems not a bad bet at all!

CHAPTER SIX

IMPLICATIONS FOR SUPERVISION OF COUNSELING THEORY AND TECHNIQUE

Very little analysis has been undertaken of what happens to the student teacher psychologically during his practice teaching. Little has been written about the way in which the beginner acquires knowledge about, and takes on behavior appropriate to, the role of teacher which differentiates him in that role from the private (personal and nonprofessional) person he is.[1] We do know from the turnover rate that a great deal happens psychologically to beginning teachers and that much of it is apparently very negative. This is particularly so in the case of those who begin teaching in urban schools. This chapter will focus on the personal and emotional dimension of the problems encountered by the teacher-in-training, and on a method of supervision responsive to these problems. Throughout the chapter, however, and in a concluding sec-

[1]By contrast, rather substantial psychological and sociological study has been made of social workers in training, "boys in white," and of "laymen to lawmen."

tion, many implications for the supervision of experienced teachers will be drawn. Our concern is not with the issues of professional training in the abstract but with how these problems may be experienced and responded to by the student teacher himself.

TEACHING AND THE PERSONAL DEVELOPMENT OF THE TEACHER

The traditional assumption in supervision is that analysis of teaching should be restricted to the issues of curriculum and content, pedagogy and pupil response and should avoid involvement with the "personal" response and experience of the teacher.[2] This chapter will argue that supervision *must* be responsive to the teacher as a person. In light both of the ambiguity of research on the relationship between the teacher's personality and his practice and of supervision's usual emphasis on teacher behavior rather than teacher personality, why get involved with what the teacher *is*?[3] Though it may seem contradictory, the basic reason is the unproved assumption that what the teacher is personally affects what he does and what pupils do (i.e., learn). Both research and supervision, in the writer's view, have been unproductive in analyzing this interaction. What is known is, to put it mildly, neither exhaustive nor constraining.

Long involvement in supervising teachers makes it clear that traditional supervision is based on too restricted a conception of what and how a student teacher learns in his practical training. Learning to teach requires the student to change what he does. He must change, or learn, such instrumental behaviors, or teaching skills, as lesson planning, questioning

[2] Cogan states the position clearly in regard to clinical supervision: "[The supervisor] must be concerned with behavior, not deep-lying patterns of personality . . . [He] must forge a cutting edge of supervision that will cut to the truth of the actual teaching performance and the results of the teaching, without cutting into the self of the [teacher]" (Cogan 1961, p. 8).

[3] See, for example, Getzels and Jackson (1964).

and classroom management techniques. Learning to teach also requires, in simplest terms, that he change what he is. He must, for example, acquire new understandings about the significance of his particular discipline, the school as an institution, its expectations of the teacher, children, the teacher's use of authority and, in general, himself.[4]

Student teachers differ in the kind of change which is necessary. The change required may involve personal philosophy, teaching skill or emotional understanding of children or oneself. Student teachers vary, too, in their ability or willingness to change. But most must change if they are to teach, to meet both their own standards and those of the school. The majority of teachers are made by their experience, not born.

In some trainees, indicated changes in teaching behavior seem not to occur because of lack of "personal" change. For example, the student may not want to "discipline" children or adolescents. As one trainee put it, "I just wasn't brought up that way." Another student has the opposite problem:

I gather that they [pupils] aren't any worse with me as a student teacher than they are with Mr._____ [critic teacher], but I'm nastier about it than he is. I just don't like that sort of messing around! You know, if you get this far, you've always been at some point a good student and I was, oh, a sweet child at school and I always paid attention (laughs) . . . So it's probably more my adjusting to the present school system's standards of "permissiveness." There was never any permissiveness at home and, uh, I grew up, you know, that way. There was no whining, there was no—you know—you asked and it was said 'no' or it was said 'yes' and that was it. There was no interrupting of adults. There was not this sort of thing. So,

[4]It should not be surprising that the increasingly select students entering teaching experience both profound intellectual reservations about the school as an institution and emotional conflict about teaching. Their high ability gives them career options; conditions in the public schools occasion criticism even within the "establishment," and the issue of the "right" curriculum, type of instruction and teacher is unresolved.

I . . . I have to become more flexible, too, in things I didn't even think about before. I never realized that I was—that these things were in me so subtly.

Another problem might be the negative attitude, or limited initial sense of personal responsibility, to non-college-preparatory children suggested in the comment, "I set out to crucify those kids on the cross of Yale's standards." By contrast, acute problems of change in both attitude and behavior face the well-intentioned young middle-class white teachers whose objective, in the words of a former superintendent in New Orleans, "is essentially to sit on the floor and love poor black kids," but who are expected by their students' parents to provide discipline, rigorous academic training and marketable vocational skills. Changes in this area of personal intentions, attitudes, assumptions and feelings with regard to teaching can be as important to successful or satisfying teaching as are changes in knowledge of content or instructional method.

From this background, then, the idea emerges that change in a student teacher's intentions, perceptions and feelings about teaching children can affect his teaching behavior. Whether behavior *is* subject to cognitive control (i.e., to changes in the individual's perception and ideas relative to his experience) or is altered primarily by the environmental effects of one's acts is an unresolved issue in both American and Soviet psychology (Bruner 1962, pp. 132ff.). Nevertheless, it is not a new idea in teacher training or supervision that one can think oneself into a new way of acting. This is, for example, a basic assumption of clinical supervision. As already noted, it is assumed that most teachers in training do change their personal plans, perceptions and ideas about teaching as well as their classroom behavior (Molchen 1967). The writer's position is that it is important that this process be made conscious and that it develop a specifically professional cast. This would have at least two levels of effect:

1) increased ability to understand and control the personal and professional problems caused by student teaching, and 2) related changes in the quality of the teaching performance.

THE PROCESS OF BECOMING A TEACHER: A FRAMEWORK FOR SUPERVISION

Let us first discuss more specifically the kinds of problems student teachers confront and what happens psychologically to the student teacher as he begins teaching. We will borrow functional ideas from sociology and psychology. The sociological viewpoint is a useful way of talking about the school and the job of teacher; ego-psychology offers *one* set of ideas and terms for the discussion of teacher personality. Ego-psychology is basic, also, to the theory and practice of ego counseling, the application of which to supervision constitutes a major focus of this chapter.

Developing a Personal Philosophy of Teaching

The individual has to see, think and behave in new ways as he begins to teach. He has to decide a) what is expected of him as a teacher, by whom and with what consensus and authority, b) which external job requirements and personal objectives he is to realize in the position, and c) how most effectively to attain these objectives. The first phase of becoming a teacher might be described as learning what one is expected to *do* and to *be* as a teacher. It is important to note that the school makes explicit assumptions about what a teacher does and is, and that these expectations are shared by people in positions crucial to the beginner: the supervisor responsible for his student teaching, the school principal, the university professor of education and others.

A second phase involves developing for himself ideas and plans about what *he* will do and be as a teacher. These ideas may have a variety of sources—the beginner's own experience of school and teachers, his formal education, his values and his reaction to the school and teaching as he now experiences it.

The typical beginning teacher's ideas are often discrete, conflicting and personally inconsistent. Contradictions seem especially likely between the student's view of himself and objectives for his teaching and the expectations of the school or of the teacher education program. Such discrepancies can give him trouble. The English major may expect to lecture on the heritage of English literature, while the school requires him to teach grammar to students in a business curriculum, and his methods instructor raises questions about content justification (why teach grammar?) and the translation of what is to be taught into "pupil behavior" terms. The teacher's relationship to students and the school is another source of conflict. The student teacher often values interpersonal relationships with the children above discipline. He may want to dissociate himself from arbitrary, judgmental—or *any*—exercise of teacher authority. He may not see the order of the school as his problem. Such feelings may be especially precipitated in white middle-class teachers by contact with poor black children in city schools, but the same issues prevail in suburbia.

The Emotional Challenge of the Classroom

Varying degrees of intellectual conflict, and of motivation, may be expected among beginning teachers. Most teachers-in-training can handle both the academic requirements of the training program and these first, essentially academic, contradictions regarding the role of the teacher. But the "reality-shock" of the practice classroom introduces emotionally "real" challenge and conflict. The student's previous integrity is challenged. And the challenge is not merely an intellectual debate over ideas and beliefs—he, as a person, is directly engaged and tested in an occupational, *doing* context. For many teacher trainees this may be the first major commitment of themselves to the world of work—a new, adult and ultimately central occupational environment.

Teaching tests one's intellectual ability to plan, flexibly manage and control a group learning situation and demands such interpersonal capacities as the ability to relate to, yet discipline, children. Evidence suggests that the experience of student teaching causes anxiety regarding discipline and being liked by pupils, that whatever anxieties exist at the start of student teaching tend to be relatively as intense at its completion and that anxiety with regard to discipline may, in fact, increase (Travers *et al.* 1952). Put another way, the requirements of the job frequently exceed the student teacher's immediate capacity to cope or adapt. It is this gap, between the requirements of the job, the student's self-expectancies and his actual performance as a teacher, which creates stress. This situation may be reflected most clearly in those students whose personality dispositions make such a crisis situation especially meaningful emotionally (Lindemann 1956). The effects of such stress are probably curvilinear with regard to one's teaching; too little stress can result in lackadaisical, unconcerned teaching while too much stress can cause frightened, rigid teaching behavior. Anxiety does, however, motivate change

Common Defenses Against Anxiety

An anxiety-laden situation often evokes an individual's characteristic defenses. Reactions exhibited in student teaching may be:

Intellectualization—an excited lecture in what is to the children, in the abstraction of its ideas and vocabulary, essentially a foreign language.

Reaction formation—"I really like every kid in the class."

Suppression or denial—"There's no problem of discipline."

Rationalization—"Ideologically, I'm a progressive."

Projection—"What can you expect with a curriculum like that?"

Regression or dependency—"Tell me what to do."

It is possible to conceptualize teaching behavior, particularly beginning practice, in terms of such characteristic emotional responses:[5]

Practice provides an opportunity to analyze the characteristic defenses which a teacher employs in the face of stress, to test the appropriateness of these defenses, and to develop rational, controlled behavior to handle the stress conditions. In many ways the situation is similar to the process of psychotherapy, though with less intent to change the basic personality; the examination of the appropriateness of reactions and defenses, the inquiry into why things are this way, the achievement of emotional insight, and the search for new adaptive behavior congenial to the emotional growth that takes place" (Shaplin 1961, p. 35).

Thus it is possible for a realignment of the beginner's objectives to occur. Both new "whys" and new ways of responding in the classroom are possible. At this turning point, too, the beginning teacher may be particularly open both to self-analysis and to discussion with others about his teaching attitudes and behavior.

Personal Role Definition

A third, crucial phase in learning to be a teacher may be characterized by its central challenge—the process of personal role definition. In Chapters One and Four it has been argued that helping teachers develop personally is a crucial function for supervision. Primary emphasis was put on developing the

[5]Particularly if Allport's significant qualification is introduced: "We have become so impressed with their frequency of operation, that we are inclined to forget that the rational functioning of the proprium is capable also of yielding true solutions, appropriate adjustments, accurate planning, and a relatively faultless solving of the equations of life" (Allport 1955, p. 46).

teacher's "professional identity" and helping the teacher find and maintain an autonomous, individually unique teaching style consistent with the desired learning outcomes of the curriculum. "Personal role definition" means the development of distinct, individual and consistent concepts of oneself-as-teacher and of characteristic ways of teaching. In essence, this definition takes into account the student teacher's struggle to synthesize many personal and job factors into a unique personal and professional role identity.

[Role definition involves] the individual's attempt to structure his social reality, to define his place within it and to guide his search for meaning and gratification. Role definition is, in this sense, an *ego-achievement*—a reflection of the person's capacity to resolve conflicting demands, to utilize existing opportunities and create new ones and to find some balance between stability and change, conformity and autonomy, the ideal and the feasible, in a complex environment (Levinson 1959, p. 177).[6]

To emphasize the process of defining oneself as a teacher is not to argue against the view that intellectual resources, command of the subject and instructional skills are basic to successful teaching. It is simply to suggest that an important additional factor in the teacher's effectiveness, and in his commitment to teaching, is the degree to which he finds in the job ways to express significant personal motives and needs. In simplest terms, the assumption is that the self or the person is involved in teaching whether one is a "master teacher" or a "beginner," whether the teaching is successful or ineffectual.

[6]Levinson's argument that role definition can be understood as an ego achievement is an assumption crucial to this chapter. Two views of the process of becoming a teacher—the sociological and psychological—rather than being juxtaposed as in clinical supervision, are bridged. A significant justification for studying the personal experience and adaptation of the student teacher—both conceptually and in terms of its relevance for supervision—is implicit in this argument. The case for ego psychology as the relevant psychological theory will be returned to later.

A further point is that finding in teaching ways to express, professionally, significant personal motives and needs not only *involves* but *changes* the person. The development of a professional identity means, psychologically, a complex and often profound process of personal change; change, that is, in the individual's intentions, perception, assumptions and behavior. Such personal change can have as much relevance for empirical study or for supervision as does the student's learning about curriculum issues or instructional method.

EGO-COUNSELING'S RELEVANCE TO THE SUPERVISION OF TEACHING

If finding ways to express, in teaching, significant personal motives and needs involves and changes the individual, then supervision, in addition to providing for discussion of curriculum and pedagogical issues, should find ways to respond significantly to the teacher as a person.

It may be asked why we look to theories or methods of counseling to accomplish this. And, more specifically, why we look to the theory and method of ego-counseling.

WHY COUNSELING?

The general arguments for using a counseling framework in the supervision of the student teacher, some of which are implicit in the preceding section, are:

1. As Shaplin (1961) points out, the objectives and procedure of supervision resemble in many ways the process of psychotherapy, although with less intent to change the basic personality of the student teacher.". . . examination of the appropriateness [of the teacher's] reactions and defenses, the inquiry into why things are this way, the achievement of emotional insight, and the search for new adaptive behavior congenial to the emotional growth that takes place" (p. 35) is as cogent an argument for counseling student teachers as it is for their supervision.

2. The student teacher brings the intellectual and emotional stress which can be caused by practice teaching to his supervisory conferences. As Cogan emphasizes, "Supervision deals with people in their most vital and vulnerable aspects." Supervision, however, typically tends *not* to do this. Counseling theory and practice are relatively more attuned to the "most vital and vulnerable" in the individual.

3. The view in teacher education that self-evaluation is important to professional growth would tend to orient supervision toward counseling. The writer believes that the teacher wants and has a right to participate in analyzing and controlling his own professional behavior. Counseling puts heavy emphasis on the client's responsibility for analysis and solutions.

4. The importance of self-knowledge—as distinguished from self-evaluation of professional behavior—to the student teacher has considerable support in the literature. (See, for example, Biber (1956) and Symonds (1955).) This emphasis would seem to imply an argument for counseling as a function of teacher training (though not necessarily as part of supervision), especially insofar as counseling is an educational process directly concerned with greater self-knowledge. Indeed, a number of training programs, particularly those preparing teachers to work with poor black or white children, provide group sensitivity training or similar experience.

5. It might seem logical to suppose that the effectiveness of the supervision of the student teacher will vary, in important part, with the degree to which this function is both individualized and intensive. There is supporting evidence for this idea from related professions (Mosher 1962). Counseling concentrates on intensive one-to-one interaction designed to effect change in the individual's behavior.

Rather than asking, "Why ego-counseling?" we might ask, "Why *not* psychotherapy, client-centered therapy or some other method of counseling?" There is a considerable literature on the relevance of psychotherapy for teachers in training and in service (Rogers 1962). Generally, however, psychotherapy has remained auxiliary to the academic and student teaching program, its principal function being the referral and treatment of student teachers who find the crisis situation of practice teaching relatively overwhelming. The status of psychotherapy reflects the fact that it is typically a medical treatment procedure, concerned with more intensive change in basic personality structure than is feasible or necessary in the training of a majority of student teachers. Beginning teachers represent, by and large, a "normal" population. Their problems are more a matter of developing occupational behavior and defining themselves as teachers than of changing maladaptive or neurotic personal behavior.

Practical limitations to the use of psychotherapy lie in the economics of teacher training—the time and cost usually involved in psychotherapy—in the uneven availability of psychiatric services and in reservations about psychiatric referral on the part of teacher educators and the trainees themselves.

The client-centered counseling approach originated by Carl Rogers is also essentially a therapy procedure. Rogers attaches critical importance to the quality of the relationship between counselor and client in effecting a therapeutic result, and emphasizes the counselor's sharing of the personal world of the client, a nondirective kind of treatment and the importance of the client's feelings in contrast to intellectual processes. Rogers has indicated, however, that the client-centered approach pertains directly to the training of teachers and their supervision:

I have worked with troubled college students, with adults in difficulty, with 'normal' individuals . . . I have endeavored to make use of the learnings from my therapeutic experience in my interactions with classes and seminars, in the training of teachers . . . in the clinical supervision of psychologists, psychiatrists, and guidance workers . . . I have come to the conclusion that one learning which applies to all of these experiences is that it is the quality of the personal relationship which matters most . . . which determines the extent to which this is an experience which releases or promotes development or growth. I believe the quality of my encounter is more important in the long run than is my scholarly knowledge, my professional training, my counseling orientation, the techniques I use in the interview (Rogers 1962, p. 416).

The relevance of client-centered therapy to a more comprehensive method of supervising teachers is, then, an open and important question. Bennington's work, discussed in Chapter Three, is to date the most significant adaptation of client-centered procedures to supervision.

WHY "EGO-COUNSELING"?

Ego-counseling rests upon the theory, basic to ego psychology, that the normal individual's behavior is organized by the ego. The structure of the ego—the individual's values, his personal traits, attitudes and assumptions—and the ego functions of perception, thought, planning and action in regard to "reality" problems, are the focus of both ego theory and the method of ego counseling.

A distinguishing feature of ego-counseling is the importance it places, theoretically and in practice, on "secondary process" —that is, the ego functions of planning, logical thinking and problem solving. Ego-counseling recognizes the "vital realm" of impulse and feeling, the fact that some behavior may be motivated by unconscious factors and "the enormous subtlety and importance of personal relationship in all psychological treatment processes" (Hummel 1962, p. 468). Ego-counseling is not a narrow or naive (that is, pre-Freudian) rationalism. It assumes, however, that secondary processes can be "functionally autonomous" within the personality structure, that "the rational functioning of the . . . [ego] is capable . . . of yielding true solutions, appropriate adjustments, accurate planning, and a relatively faultless solving of the equations of life" (Allport 1955, p. 46).

It is with the quality of ego as *organization* . . . with the increasing capacity of the . . . individual to perceive reality in more accurate terms, to differentiate and impose more complex meanings on reality . . . to control impulse in the light of anticipated consequences, to mediate conflicting dispositions, to employ rational considerations in solving problems, to pursue more remote goals in a dependable way . . . it is to foster aspects of ego-organization such as these that the ego-counselor participates [with] the counselee (Hummel 1962, p. 468).

Ego-counseling is, thus, concerned with intellectual analysis —with the individual's thinking. It focuses on the *personal condition* of the individual by reasoning about and revising personal (rather than abstract) reality problems, plans and actions. A concern with cognitive theory follows logically. In short, ego-counseling derives support both from the ego theory of Allport, Hartman and Bronfenbrenner and from the "fruitful promise for counseling theorists in the work of Piaget, Bruner, Rapaport, George Kelly, and of other investigators into the nature of thinking" (Hummel 1965, p. 97).

Let us look more closely at the principles, both theoretical and practical, which follow from ego-counseling's emphasis on thinking activity.

The Focus of Ego-Counseling

Discussion in ego-counseling tends to focus on:

1. Careful appraisal by the individual of himself (as he is and as he would like to be) in his situation. This appraisal elicits, and subsequently measures progress by, "a set of counselee constructs with relation to some significant role of situation in reality" (Hummel 1965, p. 97). Such a "significant role," quite obviously, is that of the teacher.

2. The relation of the individual's present actions to the realization of his objectives—that is, the connection between means and ends.

3. The consideration of obstacles, both personal and situational, to such aims.

4. The development of revised ways of thinking about, and acting in, the situation of being a teacher.

Assumptions About the Counselee

In ego-counseling, the counselee is seen "as 'investigator,' as . . . analyst of certain aspects of his personal condition" (Hummel 1965, p. 96). The term "analyst" is used not in its special psychoanalytic sense, but to suggest the importance placed by this counseling method on cognitive process. A related assumption is that "the counselee is willing and capable to analyze and to cope with those concerns which brought him into counseling" (Hummel 1962, p. 467). The essential responsibility for both analysis and solutions rests with the individual. The counselor offers his collaboration in the analysis. (It is worth noting that these assumptions support the principle that self-evaluation by the teacher has important potential for furthering his professional growth.)

Conditions Guiding the Counseling Approach

Ego-counseling's emphasis on thinking about one's personal situation is adhered to in several characteristic ways:

1. Sector. Ego-counseling has adapted Deutsch's notion of "sector" as a way of controlling the topics considered in treatment (Deutsch 1949). Discussion is focused on the individual's thinking with regard to an important and "real" role or situation such as teaching. The sector may still be defined broadly as, for example, the wide range of attitudes, personal reactions and behaviors elicited by teaching; it may be as particular as the inability to discipline or motivate a given class; it may center on a concrete incident such as a difficult parent conference or a disagreement with a department chairman, or it may be a relatively abstract discussion of the role of the school administrator and the teacher's projections of himself to such a future role. Assume, by way of illustration, that the sector is classroom behavior and its personal and situational determinants. Such limits help the supervisor to steer between, on the one hand, insensitivity or inaction with regard to personal variables affecting the teaching and, on the other hand, the intensive efforts at reorganization of the basic personality of the teacher which characterize psychotherapy.

2. No "Deep" Interpretation. Typically, psychological assessment—that is, projective testing—is not used in this method, and minimal attention is given to unconscious meaning in the individual's statements. "Deep" or symbolic interpretation of what he says is avoided, and discussion remains close to the individual's level of awareness. There is an underlying assumption that dealing with external problems can affect what is not conscious. These points represent major distinctions between this method and Freudian or psychoanalytic practice.

In brief, an ego-counselor will respond as intensively as possible from his own preconscious . . . to the cues and symbols in the counselee's talk. . . In his effort to understand the counselee, he considers no area of thinking about human behavior, including the psychology of the unconscious, to be *arbitrarily* outside his province. . . In his communication of understanding to the counselee, however, he is likely to refrain from interpreting symbolic meanings (Hummel 1961, p. 41).

In contrast to analytic therapy, the ego-counselor *does not* deal with unconscious material which may affect the individual's teaching. In contrast to Cogan's concern with "supervision which will cut to the truth of the actual teaching performance and the results of the teaching without cutting into the self of the intern," ego-counseling *does* deal with the full range of *conscious* personal response to teaching—both intellectual and emotional.

3. Abridgement of Relationship. The objective in ego-counseling is that the individual think through and make decisions about a problem in reality. It is assumed that he is sufficiently mobile and free from personality disturbance to do so, and in a relatively short time. The individual's own thinking is the primary agency of change, rather than the relationship between the counselor and the individual. Illustrative of this emphasis are the "abridgement" of relationship in ego-counseling (an average number of conferences being five), the priority given by the counselor to "the counselee's questions and choices [rather] than to his satisfaction in their relationship" (Hummel 1965, p. 97), and the definition of the counseling relationship "primarily as a means or a vehicle" (p. 97). The reader will note important differences with regard to relationship between ego-counseling and, for example, client-centered counseling, and particularly with the deliberate use of the transference relationship in analytic therapy.

Other constraints on relationship are involved. For example, the limited number of contacts keeps many people from overinvesting in the relationship with the counselor. The counselor, too, engages in restraining behaviors such as structuring statements, reflections or interpretations which underline the individual's responsibility in the process; the topic may be changed when the individual seems to be moving toward a too-intense involvement, and important themes may be avoided.

An ego-counselor respects the power and the subtlety in the counseling relationship. . . From their affiliation the counselee may derive substantial comfort and strength. Yet in an ego-counselor's philosophy of practice, love is not enough. Beyond the counseling hour are circumstances in the counselee's life which require analysis and resolution. There are facts to be surveyed, feelings to be clarified, alternatives to be considered, decisions to be made and acted upon (Hummel 1965, pp. 96–97).

The "Right" Client for Ego-Counseling

Ego-counseling was first used with a population of bright but underachieving high school boys. The general criteria for selecting "clients" have already been noted: a willingness and ability on the individual's part to think through aspects of his personal condition; relative freedom from severe neurotic defense, and sufficient mobility to change attitudes and/or behavior in short-term contact. In short, ego-counseling is most applicable to the educational, vocational and personal problems of normal individuals (those without symptoms of pervasive personal disturbance).

Implications for Ego-Counseling Method

The importance given in ego-counseling to reasoning about the individual's personal situation is reflected, as well, in what the counselor characteristically does. A key responsibility of the counselor is "an unremitting effort to understand the counselee and to impart back his understanding" (Hummel 1965, p. 98). *Reflection*—"a most powerful technique for communicating understanding" (p. 98)—is one of the distinctive techniques the counselor uses to communicate his understanding. The focus, however, is primarily on restatement by the counselor of the meanings implicit in what the individual says, as they bear on consequences, planning and possible actions, rather than on reflection of the individual's feelings per se. Particularly significant is the use by the counselor of *questioning, interpretation*—"a construction of events in the experience of the counselee which the latter has not already himself formulated" (p. 102)—and *confrontation*, "a particular form of interpretation in which the counselor proposes that contradiction exists between two aspects of client thinking or overt behavior" (p. 102). Again, it is consistent with the importance placed by ego-counseling on analysis and thinking activity by the counselee that the counselor, too, is relatively active and objective intellectually.

Ego-counseling in particular "retains a place for both phenomenological and objective viewpoints in the same methodological system" (Hummel 1962, p. 476). In short, there is a place for the client's thinking, the counselor's thinking and objective evidence. A discussion in which a supervisor explores and pursues with a teacher solutions to instructional problems which the supervisor strives to understand both objectively and as the teacher sees them is very close in methods and goals to ego-counseling. Talk about one's self, the actual situation and self-in-situation are integral to ego-counseling. Similar discussion is equally as important in supervision.

Analysis, Synthesis and Action—Central Concerns in Ego-Counseling

How an individual sees, thinks about and acts in an actual role or relationship is, then, of central importance in this method (pp. 467 and 477–479). "Analysis" is a broad term, referring both to perceptual differentiation of the role or relationship and to the complex reorganization and synthesis of ideas in which the individual must engage actively to make new sense out of his experience.

In cognitive terms, ego-counseling may be said to help the counselee *to attain* a revised set of intentions . . . of "personal constructs" with reference to a defined sector. . . Ego-counseling is intended to achieve change not merely in specific behavior . . . but in the complex of meanings and organizing principles which guide the counselee in his transactions within the sector (p. 479).

Rehearsal for actual behavior is an integral part of ego-counseling. It is integral because tryout is an essential aspect of secondary process, because the educational institutions in which counseling is typically practiced are appropriately concerned with practical effects and in order "to establish a

sufficient conception of counseling as an educative function"
(p. 480).

A BLUEPRINT FOR AN APPLICATION OF
EGO-COUNSELING TO SUPERVISION

An abstract for an application of ego-counseling to the problems confronting the beginning teacher follows. It embodies the process of analysis, synthesis and action discussed above. The purpose is to summarize the preceding arguments and to establish, at least theoretically, the relevance of ego-counseling as a way of responding to the problems of becoming a teacher. The reader should be alert to the danger of oversimplifying both counseling and supervision strategies and the unsystematic and only partly conscious process of development in the beginning teacher.

SECTOR: PROBLEMS CONFRONTED BY THE BEGINNING TEACHER.

Phases in the Supervision	*Dominant Issues*	*Representative Questions Which the Teacher May Ask or Be Led to Analyze*
Analysis	A. Job expectations: on the part of the school, the school supervisor, the college training program	What is expected of me as a teacher by the school, the school supervisor, the university training program? What am I supposed to be as a teacher—what attributes are expected? What am I supposed to do, in terms of curriculum and pedagogy?
Systematic appraisal by the teacher of A (the job expectations)	B₁. Personal role definition	What are the objectives I want to accomplish in teaching? What do

Phases (cont.)	Dominant Issues (cont.)	Representative Questions (cont.)
B (personal objectives in teaching) and C (self-image) will lead to:		*I* want my teaching to be? With what interest and intensity? (How much am I personally committed to and responsible for these objectives?)
	C. Self-image	What and who am I? What are my present competencies to cope with teaching? What personal assets and what limitations will affect what I am expected, or want, to accomplish in teaching (i.e., A & B₁)?
Confrontation/ Analysis	D. Discrepancies between A (job expectations), B (personal intentions) and C (current personal assets and limitations)	Are there contradictions between A, B₁ and C? How do I react to these incompatibilities (e.g., by denial, distortion, avoiding, personal resistance to the job expectations, defensively)? With what feelings and anxiety? With what consequences for my teaching?

(The supervisor, during this phase, may make interpretations or tentative hypotheses about the problem being considered by the teacher. These may relate to A (i.e., the school or classroom reality). For example, the supervisor might report information enabling the teacher to make comparisons of his classroom performance with that of other teachers. Similarly, the supervisor might relate his hypotheses to specialized knowledge about the process of teaching, pupil differences, etc. The supervisor may also give interpretations or tentative hypotheses about B_1 and C. Such interpretations about the teacher's assumptions, ways of reacting to children, etc., would remain close to the latter's level of awareness.)

Reorganization and synthesis leading to a revised set of intentions (i.e., a revised B_1) in light of analysis of A, B, C and D	B_2. Revised personal model(s) for teaching (an emerging "professional self")	How do I select, and justify, the curriculum or content? What are alternative objectives for my teaching (given differentiation of A, B_1, C and D)? What is the synthesis?
	E. Development of behavior making attainment of B_2 possible	In what ways do my present efforts and attitudes contribute to the probable realization or failure of B_2? How might I change my assumptions and behavior to make them more functional to B_2?
Action	F. 1 Rehearsal for action	How might I act given particular situations? (How can I respond to a particularly troublesome pupil or class? How might I "turn on" disinterested or

Phases (cont.)	Dominant Issues (cont.)	Representative Questions (cont.)
		disaffected children? How might I plan or present material more clearly and cogently?)
	2 Situational tryout	What were the results when I tried F_1 in the classroom?

SUMMARY AND IMPLICATIONS

The teacher's perceptions, his assumptions and how he feels all affect what he says and does with students. Teaching behavior is an intellectual and emotional expression of the person. The practical consequence is that supervision is incomplete unless it can deal with the person and with the assumptions and feelings his classroom talk and behavior express.

It has also been argued that the teacher himself can and should be *the* significant participant in the analysis of his teaching and that by so doing he can acquire increased understanding and effectiveness in his teaching. This position reflects a clear value commitment: that the teacher wants and has a right to participate in analyzing and controlling his own professional behavior. A second reason for the emphasis on the teacher's personal analysis of classroom events is the absence of any valid, reliable evidence available to supervision as to who the effective teacher is or what is the "right view" of most curriculum and instructional issues. Further, there seems good reason to believe that supervision will have little effect on the process of instruction or student learning unless the teacher accepts and understands the analysis of his teaching.

We are not, however, simply arguing for more significant self-evaluation of professional behavior by beginning or experienced teachers. (This idea is not new in supervision; an *effective method* for such self-analysis of teaching is new.) Nor is the argument in this chapter distinctive in its assumption that it makes sense for the teacher to think about his teaching—to employ rational capacities to solve teaching problems. Clinical supervision is based on the same premise. The distinction lies in what is thought and talked about. The method of supervision discussed here is particularly sensitive to the fact that beginning teachers, at least, do not think about their teaching "abstractly" or objectively. Curricular and pedagogical issues can have distinctly personal overtones. Our contention is that supervision must be able to assist the teacher in making simultaneous curricular, pedagogical and personal meaning out of the experience of practice. (Teachers must, of course, be free *not to talk about themselves* if they choose. The problem in supervision has traditionally been the reverse: the teacher has usually been unable to talk about his personal responses when he wanted to.)

A compelling rationale for dealing with the intellectual and emotional responses of the teacher is based on evidence that talking about these responses in a structured way can generalize to measurable improvement in teaching behavior.[7] There is an equally compelling, if more romantic, reason. Our experience is that beginning teachers may make a great deal of meaning from their first contact with practice—that exceedingly significant personal and professional learning can occur

[7] The writer supervised two groups comprising 17 student teachers in this manner. Independent ratings of their teaching performance increased 1.82 grade points on a 7-point rating scale. Their average grade at the end of six preliminary weeks of student teaching was B. A five-month internship in the public schools followed, during which time they were supervised by the method of ego-counseling. The average grade at the end was A—. A subsample of 7 student teachers who were particularly ineffective in the first six weeks increased 2.5 grade points in the subsequent internship—from an average grade of B— to an average grade of A—. Both changes were highly significant statistically. The improvement in rated teaching performance also was significantly greater than that of an analogous group of student teachers receiving conventional supervision.

at this point. Teachers are made, or broken, by practice in ways more complex than supervision, education or psychology have realized. The supervisor, almost uniquely among teacher educators, can be relevant to, and affect, this process of professional and personal learning. This is not to say that the supervisor is currently relevant or effective in this way, but that he is most closely associated with the one experience in the teacher's education which is, by definition, most decisive.

The argument that supervision must respond to the personal, the idiosyncratic and the expressive in teaching can be summarized in a more formal statement. Developing adaptive behavior and defining oneself as a teacher involve a learning process and an area of attention distinguishable, but not separate, both from considerations of curriculum and method and from change in the basic personality structure of the teacher. Distinctive to this process are *new* learnings: new teaching behavior and new concepts of oneself as a teacher. Supervision must understand this process of personal growth in the teacher and offer support to it.

It is important to emphasize again what is *not* implied in this chapter. The proposal for a more comprehensive conception and method of supervision is not intended to imply that proficiency in curriculum content and teaching method is not a necessary objective of supervision. Nothing we have said should be taken as an argument against subject-matter or pedagogical competence, or against supervisory analysis of these areas.[8] The method discussed here is more "compre-

---

[8]Since we know so little about the components of effective teaching, it would seem only common sense to avoid a limited or confining model of effective teaching behavior. This is another reason the method of supervision outlined here gives as much emphasis to subjective criteria as to "external" standards of judging the curriculum and the effects of teaching.

[9]This raises the question of the relationship between clinical supervision and ego-counseling. The reader will recall the discussion of Blumberg and Amidon's study in Chapter Three. In particular, they found that learning about oneself, both as a teacher and as a person, occurs when the supervisor uses

hensive" in that it deals intensively with the teacher's subjective response to the objective issues of curriculum and instruction.[9]

How does the method of supervision developed in this chapter stand up to the contention that the central objective

both indirect *and* direct methods. "Direct behavior" involves giving information or opinions, directions and criticism; "indirect behavior" means accepting feelings and ideas, giving encouragement and asking questions of the teacher. The finding that effective supervision involves a high degree of both kinds of communication is entirely consistent with the writer's experience. When the relevant issues concern curriculum or pedagogy, that is what supervision should deal with. The inputs will be the supervisor's experience with the curriculum and teaching; the supervisor's technique may be direct or indirect. Clinical supervision is exceedingly useful as a model for relatively direct and didactic discussion of content and teaching. When the issues are personal or philosophical, supervision should address itself to them. Ego-counseling is a useful indirect method for hearing a person out. It is obviously also possible to deal with curriculum and teaching issues *indirectly* (as is suggested in Chapter Six) and with personal issues in a *direct* way (as is the case in clinical supervision). The general point is that a particular teacher may at one time want or need one kind of assistance, and at another time may benefit more from the other kind of help. Supervision is more effective when it is able to employ both the method of clinical supervision and the method of ego-counseling.

More specifically, the supervisor may shift from clinical to counseling supervision within the same conference. For example, a relatively didactic discussion of techniques for disciplining children may give way to a more indirect discussion of the teacher's fear of losing control of the students or his uncertain feelings about exercising authority. Such a shift is not artificial. It follows the route from *what* the teacher does to *why*, philosophically or psychologically, he is this way. What *is* artificial is to assume that there are not personal or philosophical reasons (as well as curriculum and pedagogical determinants) for his teaching behavior. Thus, when the supervisee introduces personal material, it should be honored; it may supersede at that point the supervisor's agenda. Again, this is not to say that the supervisor must become a mute, "uh-huhing" therapist. The point is to hear the teacher out. His teaching, after all, is the subject of concern. Conversely, there also must be time for the teacher to listen to the supervisor's direct clinical assessment and recommendations; they, too, express the supervisor's concern and wish to help. To know how and when to be direct or indirect is, then, a very subtle and essential part of the supervisor's craft.

and practical test · 'jy method of' upervision is its effectiveness in chaae . . the teacher's ehavior? (A digression: the necessity of iging teaching behavior—either to implement curriculu ectively or to make it consistent with empirical finding ut effective teaching—is not going to disappear as we lop more valid knowledge about curricula, instruction, i. tructional technology, teacher effectiveness and related issues. Indeed, the analysis and modification of teaching are likely to become even more important as we begin to understand the precise relationships among curriculum, teaching and student learning. Conant (1963,, for other reasons, has given a critical priority to the rôle and function of the clinical supervisor in the education of ine teacher. These pressures will facilitate the hard thinking a .d hard data which are essential if we are systematically tc' affect teacher behavior.) But to return to the issue at hand. Does it "work?" Is it practical? Evidence has been cited hat *student* eachers supervised by this method can analyze and change their attitudes and behavior in the classroom. The evidence, both about change in teaching attitudes and beha r and about the contribution of supervision to these changes, is inconclusive, but it is virtually the only evidence of wh ch the writer is aware that supervision does make a difference That, in itself, makes the method unique.

SUPERVISING EXPERIENCED TEACHERS

Is ego-counseling applicable in the supervisor's work with experienced teachers? The practical problems and personal issues confronting experienced teachers are clearly different from those encountered by beginners. The writer has, however, used these ideas and techniques with widely diverse groups of experienced teachers, counselors and supervisors. The results indicate that ego-counseling has substantial generalizability.

It might be asked whether the writer is suggesting that

ego-counseling be instituted as a formal procedure or only that certain lessons be adapted from it by supervisors. I am reluctant, given how little we know about the elements of effective teaching or about training effective teachers, to argue for "instituting" one method of supervision, whether it be clinical supervision, ego-counseling, micro-teaching, Flanders' interaction analysis or another approach. In light of the individual differences in teachers' professional development, we need to conceive of, and try out, a variety of qualitatively different ways to supervise. Having stipulated this, I will argue that we know enough about the efficacy of ego-counseling to make it available as part of the supervision program for teachers in training. As the following section will show, I also consider ego-counseling to offer significant general lessons for all supervisors.

Let us look first at some of the implications of ego-counseling for the supervision of experienced teachers, and then turn to a number of practical questions which supervisors have raised about this method. Supervision, regardless of how it is defined, involves talk between a teacher and a supervisor about teaching. The writer has observed that supervisory problems most frequently involve failures of communication. Supervisors I have known much more often pontificate, cut teachers off, lecture on their pet theories about teaching, and the like, than engage in real professional or personal communication with the teacher. One obvious suggestion which emerges from this chapter is that the supervisor observe more, listen more and talk less. The supervisor can observe more by a) getting as much information as possible on the instructional problems the *teacher* is concerned about. This supervisory function is essentially a matter of reporting, and the video or tape recorder is a useful device for "freezing" the actual data of teaching. The supervisor may observe more with the objective of b) helping the teacher identify patterns in his teaching which he himself considers effective or ineffective. The point of observation, and particularly of the supervisory analysis, might be to attempt jointly to identify logical relationships among what the teacher does, his own understanding of what he does and his ability to organize these relationships according to orderly principles. Perhaps the simplest way to observe more is c) to see two or more samples of teaching and then to compare them. The resultant comparative criteria may be more useful than is the comparison of one incident of teaching to external—that is, the supervisor's—criteria.

The writer also suggests that the supervisor listen more. It seems to be difficult for many supervisors to listen, or to comprehend, except insofar as the teacher's reply corresponds to a set of observations or an evaluation already made by the supervisor. One can oversimplify the issue by suggesting that teachers (and supervisors) are trained to talk while counselors are trained to listen, and that both professional functions—inseparable parts of the educational process—suffer from rigidity as a result. The supervisor should be able to listen acutely to several levels of communication by the teacher: his questions and problems with regard to the curriculum, instructional issues, and the expression of his personal needs and objectives. Perhaps a literary allusion may be forgiven. If supervisors could be sensitive to, or trained to hear (they do not always have to respond), Doc's three voices in Steinbeck's *Sweet Thursday*, supervisory communication, interaction and, the writer suspects, effect, could be triply powerful.

It might also be suggested that supervisors talk less. The supervisor is likely to find it more effective to talk about the teacher's perceptions (what the teacher sees) and the teacher's analysis (what he thinks is happening) than about the supervisor's own analyses. In simplest terms, one starts with the teacher as he is. Supervisors might also try assuming that the teacher, particularly if he is experienced, is relatively as perceptive as is the supervisor; they might, in the process, be surprised! *Given a colleague relationship*—a relationship of professional respect—and this is a large "given," the teacher is likely to bring up most or all of the matters the supervisor considers important. The writer has seen this happen repeatedly in work with experienced teachers. They know when they have been effective and when ineffectual! But it is very hard to convince supervisors to trust the intelligence and perceptiveness of teachers. Furthermore, supervisors frequently feel that they are not doing their jobs if they are not telling teachers how to improve.

QUESTIONS AND ANSWERS ABOUT EGO-COUNSELING

Let us now turn to the questions most frequently asked by experienced supervisors about the method of supervision just outlined, and try to answer them in terms as practical as possible. As background it should be mentioned that the ideas developed in this chapter have been discussed with a large number of supervisors working in differing situations (e.g., public school department chairmen and principals, urban teachers, independent school headmasters and department chairmen, college supervisors of student teachers and supervisory personnel in religious schools). The responses of such diverse practitioners obviously differ, but common themes do emerge. Supervisory audiences tend to be initially uncritical of the ideas and supervisory techniques which have just been described. The first enthusiasm often causes supervisors to embrace this as an all-purpose and all-powerful conception and procedure for supervision. No such grandiose claim is, or will be, made for the method. But supervisors seem to be impressed by the extent to which this method evokes significant personal responses and feelings about children, schools and teaching on the part of beginning and experienced teachers. One suspects that supervisors and teachers may identify considerably with responses which suggest questions that they themselves have asked, and may still be asking, about their profession. There is also a tendency for supervisors, a majority of whom have had little formal training or have given limited thought to this function, to be initially intimidated by a university professor who seems to have thought at length about what they do intuitively, by the psychological "magic" which may seem an ingredient in this method or by the preliminary evidence that it works. However, questions and challenges do come, in time, and they usually take the following forms:

A frequent reaction seems to be a statement to the effect that, "You may be able to supervise this way, but I have neither the training nor the disposition to deal with teachers so personally." For example, the question most frequently raised is, "Isn't training essential if one is to use this method?" The simplest answer is yes. Supervisors typically are teachers, and teachers typically do not possess or act on the framework of assumptions about learning and about the individual's responsibility in that process which are fundamental to this method. (The reader will recall the contention that teaching is an intellectual and emotional expression of the person; that supervision is incomplete unless it can deal with the person, his assumptions and feelings, and that the teacher himself can and should be *the* significant person in the analysis of his teaching and by so doing can acquire increased understanding and effect in his teaching.) Nor do supervisors usually have the training in listening or in "indirect" talk with another that *is* central to the method. Nor will all supervisors be comfortable with these assumptions. They should not feel guilty or deficient if they are uncomfortable. The method is not for them; they should concentrate on sophisticating their own styles.

For those supervisors, however, who want to be able to operate this way, a course in counseling theory and, most important, a practicum in counseling under supervision would be sufficient training. The writer has found that a significant degree of understanding and skill in this method can be developed through an intensive practicum in supervision itself. Which leads us to an essential point: training is necessary for *any* kind of supervision. It is as essential for clinical supervision as for supervision of this type. The fact that the question is so frequently raised suggests that supervision is ordinarily conceived of as an activity for which little or no special training is expected. One need not look further for an explanation of the finding that supervision typically makes no difference. There is another answer to this question about training: that the assumptions and techniques outlined in this chapter *do not* involve psychological magic. They *do*, however, make very real personal demands on the supervisor. Supervisors are human beings; were they to make themselves significantly available as people to those they supervise, many of the effects argued for in this chapter might very well follow.

A related question has to do with whether experienced teachers are as likely to talk in personal terms as are beginners. The simple answer is "probably not" but it is an error to assume that experienced teachers think or feel any less deeply about professional issues than do beginners. Once they feel safe to express their *real* thoughts and feelings in a context of personal trust, they will do so. The writer has repeatedly found this to be the case. The attractive business education teacher who feels frustrated and discouraged by not getting the same results in her second year of teaching as she did in the first; the black teacher who realizes he cannot talk with his ghetto students about their mothers and fathers because he wants to believe that they come from "nice" middle-class unbroken homes; the music teacher who leads the band at games and wins state music festivals but who feels marginal in professional status in relation both to academic teachers and to administrators and the imaginative curriculum coordinator who can't affect entrenched and conservative department heads, are but a few of the many experienced teachers who come immediately to mind. The method is, in the writer's experience, quite appropriate to their problems.

Supervisors often express anxiety about talking with teachers in a personal, open way. Given the rituals that govern communication between teachers, and within schools generally, this is not surprising. It does speak volumes about the stylized, artificial character of much of that communication. A practicum in counseling or supervision does help too, as does experience that talking with a colleague about his real attitudes and feelings as a teacher is not opening some psychological Pandora's box.

Among the technical questions raised is whether the method is appropriate only in individual supervision or whether it may be used with groups of teachers. While the technique was developed for use in individual counseling and supervision, the writer's experience is that it is applicable to teams of teachers analyzing instruction or working on curriculum. Chapter Seven discusses in detail the supervision of teachers in groups, but it may be appropriate to mention here some of the adjustments the writer makes to adapt this method to work with a group such as, say, a department or a group of supervisors-in-training. Almost by definition, the supervisor's relationship with the individual teacher is less immediately crucial than in one-to-one supervision. Conversely, it is more difficult to establish trust within the group. Revealing significant thoughts and feelings about oneself or one's teaching to colleagues is not easy. Several group meetings are usually necessary before this begins to happen. The presentation for analysis by the group of some of the supervisor's own curriculum ideas, or a sample of his teaching, can encourage openness. Certainly the agenda should be practical, focusing on the curriculum or on tape recordings of its teaching by individuals in the group. Concentrating on reformulation of the curriculum is probably the best way to get teachers to consider not only the content of what they teach but *how* they teach.

In working with groups, the writer has found it important to be quite indirect at first. One can be direct later. Groups of teachers are prone to make the supervisor act like a traditional supervisor—an expert with answers to all the questions about subject matter and teaching. The effect of responding directly to this expectation is to create the prototype of teacher and class and to make the learner dependent, a result inimical to the whole purpose of the process. But what does being "indirect" mean in the context of this method? At first, it essentially means listening—permitting the group to learn to trust one another as people and to trust their own judgment of the curricular and instructional issues being discussed. Restatements by the supervisor of the meaning or feeling expressed by individuals ("You question very much whether you really can work with this curriculum," or "You get very discouraged about ever being able to reach these children") are helpful at this stage. A consistent attempt to understand and articulate for the group the essential ideas and feelings being raised is a basic responsibility of the supervisor. It is also preferable to raise *questions* rather than to make points with the group ("How would you characterize what the teacher is doing at this stage in the lesson?" "What are the objectives of the lesson?" "What kinds of questions would you want to discuss with the teacher in analyzing the class?" "Are you saying that the material gets in the way in trying to reach these kids?").

The supervisor's attitudinal stance toward the group is important at this stage. He must be intellectually patient with teachers as they think about issues that he has considered more deeply. The supervisor should also recognize that teachers will understand what they should do before they can, in fact, do it in their teaching. It takes time and practice and support for teachers to change their classroom behavior—and more of each than is commonly understood or provided.

As a group develops trust and a working confidence in their objectives and judgments, the supervisor can become more direct. He can interpret and confront more directly ("You're lonely and afraid in the classroom." "It's frustrating not to get the results with these kids that you got a year ago." "Is it that you don't want to be simply another white adult putting black kids down?" "Isn't it that the romance about the ghetto school is over and you just want out?" "How do you square all the earlier talk about 'relevance' with this material?"). This is the stage at which there is a functional need and probably maximum effect for the supervisor's clinical judgment—*his* ideas about the curriculum or the teaching being analyzed. Blumberg and Amidon's findings about the apparent effectiveness of a combination of high indirect *and* direct supervisory behavior coincides with the writer's experience with this method. It is important to repeat that this method allows for, and even encourages, *both* indirect and direct supervision. Reiteration is necessary both because it is consistent with the way the method is used and because supervisors so often ask, "Are you ever direct?" or, "When, in this method, is the supervisor direct?"

Some specific questions about the method also need answering. One has to do with the number of supervision conferences necessary for this method to have effect. In the experimental study reported on page 136, the average number of conferences with a teacher was five; each typically lasted an hour or more. The writer's opinion is that this is minimal, and that *at least double* or triple this number of conferences with a novice or experienced teacher is necessary to produce significant or stable changes in attitudes or in classroom behavior. Obviously, there is no magic number. The experience of the teacher, the kind and complexity of the problem he brings to supervision, his attitude toward supervision or toward the supervisor and other matters will all affect the number of times they need to talk. But, in this respect, supervisory conferences are characteristically too infrequent and too unsystematic, particularly in light of the special and comprehensive objectives proposed for it in this chapter. Only as the teacher deals with his real feelings, concerns and classroom behavior is supervision able to facilitate change. Among several preconditions for this is time.

Another question has to do with the meaning of the term "sector." This idea was introduced into the method as a control on the range and intensity of personal topics discussed.

A closely related question, frequently raised, is, "Are you, in effect, practicing psychotherapy with teachers?" The simple answer is no; one of the factors which prevents us from doing so is the notion of the sector. For example, in working with a teacher experiencing discipline problems, the question of her broken engagement came up on several occasions. Had the supervisor pursued the teacher's feelings about herself, her adequacy as a woman, her relations with men, her relationship with her father, and other issues which were probably involved in this broken engagement, he would have been acting as a therapist. That is, he would have been assisting her to interpret and reorganize her present emotional experience and feelings in light of her personal history and development. By considering the broken engagement only in terms of its consequences for her feelings as a person in the classroom and her behavior there *as a teacher*, the focus is held on the job, on the present and on her performance, rather than on recapitulation or reorganization of who she is as a total person. The distinction may seem arbitrary or artificial, and it can be so. But, nonetheless, the "line" is reasonably clear and permits significant exploration of personal attitudes, feelings and experience as they relate to performance as a teacher. It may happen that the teacher needs or wants to cross the line in order to be successful or to feel satisfied. In this situation the supervisor would be scrupulous and refer the teacher to counseling or therapy.

CHAPTER SEVEN

SUPERVISING TEACHERS IN GROUPS

As supervisors in the teaching-learning process, we are concerned with helping the individual teacher achieve a fuller realization of his own professional and personal resources. While individual supervision is often invaluable, working with teachers in a group offers its own particular benefits. In the setting of a group of colleagues, the individual teacher has special opportunities to discover and to articulate aspects of himself that will enhance his teaching. The experience of sharing invites him to explore the perspectives from which he views his teaching world and to compare them with the perspectives of other members of the group. A range of alternatives emerges through discussion of these perspectives, expanding his choice of ways of responding to his students. Although the final responsibility for making sense of any experience resides in the individual teacher, mutual exploration enables him to affirm and begin to integrate his own teaching style.

I will try to show in this chapter how a group setting pro-

vides opportunities for individual learning. In group supervision, the supervisor serves as a catalyst and a resource in
the learning process. A context for learning begins to develop
as soon as group members come together; as supervisor I feel
that I have a choice between actively endeavoring to create
context or allowing context to develop by default. I choose
the former, trying to create a context which invites teachers
to learn on their own through communication with others.
Group consensus is not sought as an end in itself. Participants are encouraged to listen to and learn from one another.
Experience has led me to appreciate the value of creating a
context in which the participants, through interaction with
one another, have opportunities to pursue what they care
about. In the final analysis, no one can learn for the participants. If they are to benefit from the experience—to realize
where they are at this time in their lives—it must be in a context in which they are invited to participate actively.

A CONCEPTUAL FRAMEWORK

Our[1] responsibility as supervisors carries with it the urge to
continue to explore and to extend our own understanding of
the process of learning. In the end, we hope, our sharing with
teachers, both one-to-one and in groups, will enhance our
ultimate concern: the learning of individual students in the
classroom.

Our immediate concern, however, is the learning of each
individual within the group. Through direct interpersonal exchange we strive to perceive and respond to the unique concerns and style each teacher brings to a supervision session.
We endeavor to discover the special resources of each indivi-

[1] The use of the personal pronouns "we" and "our" throughout this chapter
expresses my personal belief that each human being, whatever his work or
profession, is continually endeavoring to communicate his caring and concern
through his personal style of expression. By the use of these pronouns, my
hope is to invite the *reader* to examine his beliefs, assumptions and values.

dual. And, through our own conduct in the group, we attempt to encourage the participants to share the same concern for one another.

Mutual learning is therefore central to this kind of supervision. As we help teachers in their work, we cannot help but learn. And through our communications with teachers we continue to discover ways to extend our services to them. In supervision and in teaching, our beliefs and assumptions about learning define the nature of the interaction through which our students learn. That is, the kinds of questions we ask, the way we ask them, the statements we formulate and the responses we give communicate our expectations and our beliefs as to how learning best takes place.

In learning about teaching we are learning about personal relationships. We are concerned with the teacher's relationships with his students—the ways in which he can and does address and communicate with his students; and with his relationship to himself—that is, how he sees himself as a teacher and how he feels about his ideas and behavior as they are involved in his teaching. In learning about teaching, therefore, we are much more personally involved—and more inescapably so—than when learning about specific subject matter. Whatever we learn about these relationships will reflect on ourselves. This kind of learning experience is what I shall refer to as *realization*.

Such learning, then, is more than cognitive. It entails complex interplay between both cognitive and emotional aspects of our being. When we learn emotionally, we often call upon our intellects to help us make sense of the experienced changes. When we learn cognitively, we react emotionally to the process and content of our learning. The one mode informs the other. Most of the time we seem to learn with mind and feelings at once. And in those moments when we experience the involvement of our whole being, our learning is richer. Learning involves the intermeshing of many facets of our person; it is difficult to distinguish neatly between learning experienced in personal growth (including psychotherapy) and learning about our conduct in the classroom.

When we learn, we create meaning. When something new happens, or when something old happens in a new way, we try in our own way to make meaning of it. This is a fundamental principle of human experience. We spend many of our waking hours developing and nurturing assumptions about ourselves and the world in which we move. Although our basic assumptions are often articulated cognitively, they tend to arise from experiences which involve strong feelings. There is constant interplay between what we assume and what we experience. When this interplay is meaningful to us, we are learning. While we are aware of many of our assumptions, some are less clearly known to us. Our beliefs and assumptions potently influence our behavior, including the ways we learn, teach and supervise. As we endeavor to create meaning, we call upon our basic assumptions to assist us. In the process, we may affirm, modify or discard old assumptions, and evolve new ones. Learning something new can reveal to us our previous assumptions, open out possibilities in the use of our person that we have not considered before or even suggest that some of our most cherished beliefs have been limited or erroneous.

Change, or the likelihood of change, seems to be inherent in such learning. Confronted with the possibility of change, we often feel ambivalent. We experience the ambivalence as a simultaneous expression of two kinds of yearning. We yearn to grow, to be different, spontaneous and, in some sense, unpredictable. At the same time, we long for stasis, security, a feeling of equilibrium and predictability. These feelings of ambivalence are intimately related to the process of learning.

Cognitive-emotional interplay, meaning-making, ambivalence: these, then, are fundamental to the kind of learning called *realization*. The process of learning entails more than taking in something new. One discovers that a shift in one's perspective on one's own behavior can offer others quite different opportunities to respond; the discovery can lead to feelings of shame for having failed to realize this possibility earlier. Examining the "how" of this relationship heightens self-awareness, and can make one doubt one's competence. In striving to make sense of the experience, one brings to bear a wealth of personal resources. When what seemed complex and beyond comprehension becomes understandable, our excitement and our urge for further exploration continue.

Each of us assumes and experiences in unique ways. While we hold many assumptions and experiences in common, it is in our uniqueness that we find richness, potency and creativity. Through understanding and claiming our own uniqueness, we can become more competent teachers. While affirming one's uniqueness is not the only factor in effective teaching, it seems to be essential to teacher competency. It may be that when we understand our own personal strivings and styles, we become freer to respond to the autonomy and individuality of others.

Moreover, since learning to facilitate others' learning is central to teacher effectiveness, an important characteristic of the competent teacher is his capacity to mobilize his own resources with versatility. Learning to draw upon his resources more creatively, the teacher may feel less vulnerable when confronted with unanticipated behavior. Such moments can be upsetting and can leave the teacher feeling naked and helpless. By becoming aware of the possible responses one may meet as well as give in the classroom, a teacher is less apt to be surprised and better able to respond with understanding to what might otherwise have seemed bizarre or frightening behavior. Accordingly, our effectiveness as supervisors depends largely on the extent to which we are attuned to the potentialities of each person we supervise. The supervisor's expertise can be brought to bear fruitfully to the extent that he perceives and responds to the unique resources of the teachers in whose training he is assisting.

Presumably, the teacher comes to supervision with a background of coursework in curricula and methodologies; he also brings a repertoire of academic and interpersonal skills acquired over his lifetime. As supervisors, our effort is to help the teacher further develop his competence in the use of these personal resources.

Supervision in a group makes it possible for multiple perspectives to be introduced; each teacher can compare issues of central concern to himself with issues of importance to his colleagues, as well as consider a variety of approaches to any one issue. He comes to understand the conflicts that result from varying needs, assumptions and purposes. Contemplating the implications of multiple perspectives on any given concern helps individuals to develop versatile repertoires from which they can come to respond to their students. The risk of falling into unexamined, routinized styles of teaching that restrict the creative potential of both teacher and student is increased if there is no setting where a teacher can become aware of his present teaching style.

GROUPS FOR PROBLEM-SOLVING, THERAPY, ENCOUNTER

The context and purposes of group discussions influence importantly the nature of what takes place. The solving of a particular problem or making specific decisions, as is done in committees, immediately brings in an evaluative element. Recognition is given the person who has the best ideas, or who does the most to help the group reach a solution for the problem. Leadership, tension release, maintaining harmony, maintaining and sustaining positions in the group, and the way these processes function to get the job done, become the focus in the problem-solving group.[1]

In settings whose focus is primarily therapeutic, the issues and concerns center on encouraging an individual to learn

[1]For detailed elaboration of group process from this perspective see Bales (1950).

about himself. Effort is directed toward self-exploration—understanding of one's own personal feelings and emotions that interfere with a more comfortable address to life in general. The subject matter is the self or person of each participant, as perceived and experienced by the others in the setting. Exploration and discovery can be deeply personal and not limited to any specific area or issue. The learning is individual and personal, although intimately shared (Rosenbaum and Berger 1963).

In "T"-groups, "sensitivity" or "basic encounter" groups, the focus is on developing skills and awareness of oneself and of the dynamics of groups, and of how the two function together as learning experience. The hope is that through participating in such an experience the person will be able to work more effectively as a group member and to live and work more fully as a member of society.[2]

GROUPS FOR TEACHERS

In supervising groups of teachers, though the focus is on issues and concerns having to do with teaching and learning, learning for the individual teacher is as personal as in "therapy" and "sensitivity" groups. Whenever personal competence is the focus of exploration, self-awareness and self-consciousness are heightened. We all prefer not to put ourselves under scrutiny because such activity threatens to confront us with experiences of shame. When such experiences are recognized as natural, legitimate and a part of the process of growth, then the context of support through sharing opens up opportunities for affirmation of one's self. When alternative ways of listening and responding become possibilities,

[2]Max Birnbaum puts it this way: "The objectives of the T-group are to help individual participants become aware of why both they and others behave as they do in groups—or, in the jargon of the professional, become aware of the underlying behavior dynamics of the group." For an extensive and cogent discussion of sensitivity training, see Birnbaum (1969, p. 82).

teachers find it challenging to try these new modes of inter-action. The knowledge that they can share the experience of trying something different with others in the group lends courage through a sense of human company. For a teacher without such support, this risk is seldom possible. The con-text of a group of colleagues where teachers can share their intimate feelings of vulnerability and fear makes it possible for teachers to share their daring more openly with their stu-dents. The subordination of all concerns to that of the better learning of students in the classroom is the basis for the group's discipline and mutual support.

CREATING A CONTEXT FOR LEARNING

The responsibility of the leader or supervisor is to create a context in which learning is most likely to occur, in other words, to try to provide a setting in which discussion, explo-ration, and discovery become possibilities. Groups don't learn; individuals do.

Optimal learning occurs when the learner assumes respon-sibility for his own learning: "responsibility" not in terms of obligation, but in the more literal sense of the ability to re-spond, especially to claim that ability as one's own. The will-ingness to claim responsibility involves a trust in one's ca-pacity to make sense, to discover meaning, to make order out of what seems to be chaos. The realization that one can do this leads to the freedom to risk feelings of loneliness that can come from being thrown back on one's own resources and judgment. To venture forth into explorations and discus-sions becomes challenging rather than frightening. The pos-sibility that meaning can and will emerge becomes a source of comfort, and lends courage to the participants' urge to learn.

It is the task of the supervisor to try to create a context which invites teachers to learn on their own, by means of interaction with one another, to discover the willingness to risk one's person in the service of one's learning. Often participants expect a supervisor to act as if he cared more about his own expertise and knowledge than about their learning.

In some respects the supervisor's task is like that of the gardener: to help create conditions which generate growth. The plant selects what it needs for growth, but too little fertilizer causes the plant to wither from lack of nutrition, while too much can burn it. The delicate balance between these two extremes is what we are seeking to achieve. This optimal blend is the *context for learning*.

THE GROUP CONTRACT

In a way, the airing and adjusting of the various hopes and expectations of group members resembles the negotiation of a complex and flexible contract. The more adequately this contract comes to reflect the expectations of every member, the more learning occurs. Various factors influence the nature of the contract and the kinds of discussions that will take place among the participants. These include such matters as the source of initiative for and formation of the group, the size of the group, the length and number of meetings and the composition of the group—that is, the field, sex and status of each member.

The Source of Initiative

These discussion groups have been most successful when the initiative to form them has come from the teachers themselves. In such instances, the teachers' commitment arises out of a desire to increase their professional competence and out of concern for their students. Obligatory participation tends to create resistance, which must then be overcome. Voluntary participants have a greater willingness to explore their personal concerns. Commitment of their time is less of an issue.

If the initiative comes from the administration, care must be taken in the way these groups are introduced. A first step would be a general discussion of such a program open to all the teachers in a school or district. This would provide an opportunity for administrators and teachers to discuss the issues that the initiation of such a program raises. Participation in the initial exploration and eventual decision forms a basis for subsequent support and interest.

The first group can then be made up of volunteers from the teaching faculty. Teachers from a single school or from several schools within a district can be invited to participate. It has been found that others become interested when they learn how the initial volunteers respond.[3] The administration can insure greater interest in and support of the program by designating time for it and perhaps by freeing the participating teachers of other duties.

Group Size

The number of participants influences both the depth and tempo of discussions. Something will happen, whatever the number; *what* happens, however, seems in part to be a function of the size of the group. In a small group of three or four, participants usually speak with reticence, as if there were no place for them to hide in moments of personal exposure. This is an important consideration in groups where discussions involve matters of intense personal concern to the participants. A large group of fifteen or more does not allow time for every member to speak to an extent comprehensive enough to be personally meaningful. This leads to feelings of frustration and can result in loss of interest and withdrawal. A group of from six to ten teachers seems to provide the optimal sense of personal involvement on the part of each participant.

The supervisor must adjust his expectations according to the size of the group with which he is working. For example, in a smaller group pauses seem to be more frequent and longer;

[3] The Bureau of Study Counsel at Harvard has conducted discussion groups with teaching fellows since 1960 on a voluntary basis. The alumni of such groups have proved to be the most successful agents of recruitment.

in a larger group, the issues under discussion change rapidly and there are often several issues on the floor at one time. What seems like confusion and "not staying on one subject" often turns out, by a kind of jelling, to be very fruitful. In too large a group, however, the apparent chaos sometimes leads to frustration and hostility among the participants, resulting in a desire to terminate the meeting or to break into smaller groups.

The Duration of Meetings

The length and number of meetings also influence discussions. Sessions which are about an hour and a half long seem to work best. Shorter sessions seem hardly to have begun when it is time to stop. And, because of the amount of energy which participants put into the discussions, longer sessions become tiring for many and concentration seems to lessen. A schedule of less than eight meetings can be worthwhile, but it limits the extent to which participants can explore their assumptions in depth.

Since these factors influence the participants, it is helpful to decide with them or to let them know at the beginning how many times the group will meet. This knowledge allows them to gauge to some extent the depth, breadth and pace of their involvement. Outside factors often determine group size and the length and frequency of supervision sessions. Each supervisor discovers for himself the optimal size and time limits for him and his groups. It is important, however, to be aware of the restrictions and opportunities posed by variations in these factors.

The Composition of the Group

If all the participants are from the same field, such as mathematics or English, the discussion can become limited to the subject matter and how it should be taught. Such discussions are, of course, important, but they are best conducted as the concern of the particular department. In groups designed to learn about the teacher-learner relationship in general, too great a focus on the participants' expertise and knowledge of the curriculum or subject matter tends to relegate exploration of process to secondary consideration. Selecting or recruiting teachers from several different fields brings the underlying teacher-learner relationship into direct consideration, enhances the opportunity to share experiences and minimizes the tendency to compete. Competition in the discussion of the educative process tends to inhibit willingness to share one's biases and beliefs. A group of both male and female teachers offers a broader spectrum of experience and resources to draw from in discussions.

Another factor that can inhibit and limit discussion is a wide difference in status among the teachers. The younger, less experienced teachers sometimes feel considerable reluctance to express their views or concerns for fear that experienced teachers will consider them irrelevant, naive or even stupid. On the other hand, the very naiveté and freshness of the novice can highlight the salience of aspects of teaching that older teachers have somehow relegated to the realm of the known and the settled. Older teachers have more at stake, more investment to risk in coming to new realizations, and they may find it painful to do so in the company of novices. In groups of nearly equal status the qualities of tentativeness and openness keep alive the possibilities for change and creativity.

Community Participation

The effort to improve teaching is such a crucial concern that it ought to elicit support from the entire school community. Participation by other service personnel, such as counselors and nurses, may provide different perspectives and data which will add to support for the students. That is, each participant can come to realize through new and different communication that other members of the school community are resources to draw upon rather than groups that compete for the welfare of the students.

Similar discussion groups might be organized for administrators to discuss issues of concern to them. Including administrators and teachers in the same group is not advisable. The presence of administrators can inhibit free discussion of the issues and concerns of teachers that are the central focus of these discussions.

If we are aware of such pressures, we become better able to sense the context out of which restricted discussions emerge. We can then help to redefine the exploration in a more generative direction.

GROUPS IN PROCESS

The opening moments of the first meeting of any group are crucial in defining the context and opportunities for learning. During the first meeting, expectations for future meetings quickly develop. If participants are called upon to speak, they will be more likely to wait to be called upon in the future. If the leader says "excellent," or in other ways praises selectively, the kinds of remarks which receive approval tend to dominate in future meetings. If no questions are recognized until the end of the session, it is likely that in future meetings participants will not interrupt the proceedings when questions occur to them (and when people hold their questions they usually do not listen as well). If, at the end of the first session, the leader summarizes the issues and concerns that he considers important, participants will thereafter tend to wait with anticipation to hear what meaning has been made of their discussion.

Summarizing also tends to discourage participants from committing themselves to a position for fear it may not coincide with the sense the leader makes of the views and ideas expressed. If at the conclusion of a session discussion of issues is left open-ended, opportunities are kept alive for continued questioning and exploring by the participants after they depart. By leaving the issues open, the supervisor risks the possibility that the teachers will fall back on their own beliefs and experiences rather than take a chance on questioning their own assumptions. Still, it seems preferable to trust in openness as a challenge to their capacity to learn and their yearning to make meaning.

THE OPENING MOMENTS

From the very first moment, then, the supervisor emphasizes by his own address a respectful appreciation of the process of discovery and of the ever-changing nature of participants' assumptions about how learning and teaching occur. Vital to the emergence of these assumptions into awareness is communication through mutual trust and support. This is *generative interaction*—everyone attending to and recognizing the complexity of the ideas and views offered, and at the same time honoring the effort and risk involved for each person as he engages in such explorations.

An enlightening illustration of the effect of the supervisor's initial approach to conducting the group is this account of a session with beginning teachers:

The first question was asked by a woman who said, "I have heard that 12-, 13-, and 14-year-olds are unteachable. What do you think?" The immediate reaction was laughter in the group.

The supervisor had a choice of several possible responses. If he had asked, "Well, what do *you* think?" she might have replied, "I don't know," and others in the group might have thought, "He's trying to get us to discuss the question, but he must know. Why doesn't he just tell us what he thinks?" If the supervisor had answered by citing research findings or by immediately expressing his opinion, he would probably have elicited further questions and established himself as a data-producing authority; he might also have initiated disagreement and challenge from other participants. By saying something like, "It depends on the child," he might have seemed to be hedging.

What the supervisor did say was, "Unteachable in what sense?" This question invited the teacher to share her feelings and thoughts about children of that age based on her experience and knowledge. The crucial word here is "unteachable," for which teachers have a range of personal meanings that emerge out of their different feelings and assumptions. Without knowing the personal context from which the question is asked, the supervisor's tendency is to answer the question from what he assumes to be the teacher's meaning. Saying "Unteachable in what sense?" seemed to communicate the supervisor's desire to hear from her. Others in the group thus had an opportunity to hear from one of their colleagues who had dared to risk raising the first question. The alternative responses mentioned would each determine a different course for the interaction that was to follow.

Careful listening to each speaker fosters the development of meaningful communication. A person who has been listened to by someone who wants to understand is more likely to listen to others in a similar fashion. When we have been heard, we are better able to hear. The supervisor interacting with individuals in the group communicates styles of listening and responding, which enables other participants to anticipate the experience of a dialogue rather than being mere witnesses of a discussion. All the participants then become actively involved in listening and responding to one another.

A context in which it is not only acceptable but expected that group members develop their capacities on their own and in communication with others usually leads to a consideration of any given issue from a variety of perspectives. When participants feel recognized, they tend to acknowledge, and to look more closely at, their basic assumptions and to go on to expand their awareness of the implications and consequences of these assumptions. It is hoped that each teacher will develop a style of his own that integrates his teacher training, classroom experiences and personal uniqueness.

USE OF CASE MATERIALS

During the first few meetings, the use of tapes and transcriptions of teaching-learning situations offers participants a common focus upon data from a single source. At the same time each person is free to explore the issue at hand from his personal perspective. Case materials provide actual instances to which teachers can respond and so begin to articulate their beliefs and assumptions about learning and teaching. In the absence of case materials, participants sometimes feel that they are being asked to talk in a vacuum, which can inhibit or delay meaningful discussion.

Often a single event in a case is interpreted in as many ways as there are participants. This seems to encourage the participating teachers to acknowledge multiple perspectives as legitimate. When he discovers the range of possible interpretations of a single event, the teacher is better able to listen and to expand his own vocabulary of responses.

Case materials also provide a source to which participants can constantly refer. Tapes and transcriptions thus help to counteract the emergence of too generalized a discussion of issues. The tapes encourage group members to ask one another such questions as, "In terms of this case, how would you act on the notion of learning you've just described?" or, "You say that girls are better readers than boys. What about the specific circumstances of this case which suggest another explanation for the boy's difficulties? Namely that . . ." or, "You've been talking about the importance of a conceptual approach to the teaching of social studies. I'm not sure that I understand the sense in which you're using 'conceptual.' It might be clearer to me if you could point to some examples."

Case materials serve another important function by establishing a basis of sharing. Each person begins with the same basic data. Venturing forth together from this common basis creates an historical perspective for the group. Each person feels himself a participant in an experience that is created and shared with the other members. They come to understand that the object of discussions is something much greater than approving or disapproving of events in the case. They come to know each other intimately. Through personally shared experiences the group develops a particular dialogue that enriches exploration and discussion.

THE FORCE OF EXPECTATIONS

In the opening moments, broad questions which are relevant for everyone invite a wide range of personal responses. The supervisor may ask, "What stood out for you in this case?" More important than the wording of these questions is the stance from which they are asked. When the leader genuinely wonders how various participants feel, when he expects a response but does not presume to know what that response will be (and cannot honestly predict it), he invites the participants to begin from where they are.

A psychiatrist was assigned to meet with a group of chronic schizophrenic patients in a series of psychotherapeutic sessions. Attendance was excellent, but time after time none of the participants spoke. Each meeting consisted of sixty minutes of silence. Puzzled by the nonparticipation of his patients, whom he expected to take the initiative, and concerned that they might gain nothing from the sessions, the psychiatrist finally approached his supervisor for advice. When the psychiatrist had described the situation, his supervisor reflected for a moment and then asked, "What do you do while the patients go off into their private worlds of fantasy?" "I sit back and fantasize, too; there doesn't seem to be anything else to do," the psychiatrist replied. As he spoke he suddenly realized the probable cause of all those silent meetings and added, "But I think I know how I might improve the situation." The next time the group met, the psychiatrist leaned forward with anticipation and looked expectantly at the various group members. By looking directly at the patients, he acknowledged their presence. They began slowly but surely to speak.

Pauses and Silences

After a broad opening question and before participants speak, there is sometimes a long pause while participants gather their thoughts. As in the group therapy incident just mentioned, the leader's attitude during this pause makes a difference. An open-ended question is valuable in that it invites participants to speak about what is most important to them, but such a question requires more time for them to respond. If the leader speaks first during the pause following his question, participants tend to assume that in this group they will not be allowed time to reflect, that a quick response is valued above thoughtful exchange.

Silences are sometimes uncomfortable. It is difficult for the leader to tune in to the meaning of them, and it can be a self-conscious time for the participants. It is my experience that they are hard at work during the pause—mulling over what has gone before, searching for words to describe intense feelings and reactions, trying to make sense out of the question posed or reconsidering previously-held assumptions. When the leader waits with anticipation to hear from group members, they usually respond out of respect for their own dignity as responsible, caring beings.

During the pause that often follows initial questions, participants may glance furtively at one another, shift uncomfortably in their seats, look quickly through case material and reexamine parts of it with concentration; before long they begin to speak, usually out of a sense of tentative involvement. Each person seems to be going through the process of ordering his thoughts and feelings so as to respond to the opening statement from his own position. When a pause occurs, the participants may feel that a hasty response from the group or an additional question from the leader is an intrusion, a violation of that moment of reflection. When we wait with interest to hear what others have to say, they usually join in; probably they too have been listening carefully to what has been said. It is this respectful attention and concern among members that is especially valuable in supervision.

As participants begin to speak, the leader—by concentrating on what they say rather than on whether they are right or wrong from a particular perspective—tries to understand the meaning each speaker is making of the subject under discussion. Because a speaker usually addresses the leader directly, a further question, or an effort by the leader to share with the group his understanding of what the teacher has said, enhances exploration. The stance of this response is an attempt to understand the assumptions the participants are endeavoring to communicate. Once the participants feel at home in the group and respond easily to one another, the supervisor can begin to enter into the discussion in other ways, too, by sharing the speculations and questions that occur to him as he listens. By this time, interaction patterns will have developed, and the group will have begun to regard the leader as a resource rather than as a final authority. This kind of interaction is especially relevant to classroom teaching. By addressing more than one person at a time, in an effort to share, and by listening carefully to others, teachers develop skills for their own classrooms.

RECOGNIZING ASSUMPTIONS

Through analysis and exploration teachers come to understand the implications of the interaction in the case under discussion. They discover how assumptions are expressed in behavior, and how assumptions and expectations, which define the learning situation, are experienced by the teacher and the learner. The following anecdote may clarify how the members of a group can help an individual discover ways that his assumptions affect his teaching:

Several years ago a tutor in English found himself in a frustrating relationship with a student who repeatedly came unprepared to tutorial. The tutor would begin each meeting by asking a number of questions about the reading assignment, in the hope of engaging the student in dialogue, but he would respond with vague, unrelated statements. The tutor became increasingly impatient and invariably ended up lecturing to the student, who picked up his pencil and studiously took notes on everything the tutor said.

The tutor, who was in a group with fellow tutors, one day in desperation shared his dilemma with them. During their discussion it was suggested that he, the tutor, had clearly defined the student's role as passive listener. The student learned that if he could wait and tolerate the opening moments of each session he would not have to read the assignment, much less risk his knowledge or understanding of the material. The only alternative left for the tutor seemed to be to lecture. After all, he was expected to "teach" the student. His sense of responsibility and commitment to his field led the tutor to try to communicate his knowledge with greater clarity and directness. The group discussion moved to speculation about the student's learning. All agreed that, while it was difficult to say what he was learning about literature, clearly he *had* learned to be passive, to wait and to consider doing his assignment unnecessary. The group concluded that in this relationship it was the tutor who was being well trained.

The group suggested that the tutor's impatience and effort to teach was robbing the student of the opportunity to learn. If he began with a question and waited for the student to tell *him* about the book, it might make a difference.

At the next tutorial meeting there were many excruciating silences as the tutor forced himself to offer time for the student to respond. He hoped the student might at least share the fact that he had not read the assignment. The tutor was able to shift from feeling frustrated to waiting, however obscure or irrelevant the student became.

At the following tutorial, however, the student had done his reading. It became evident in the dialogue that he had begun to make sense out of it for himself. The tutor reported to his group that a different relationship was emerging: the student had stopped taking notes and was actively involved and talking. What stood out most dramatically for the tutor was that whenever he began to lecture, as before, the student would automatically pick up his pencil to take notes. This became a clear signal to stop. The other discovery the tutor made was that he no longer tended to avoid the student in the dining room but welcomed his company.

EXAMINING ONE'S OWN TEACHING

As participants become more at ease discussing styles of teaching, they are invited to bring in tape recordings of their own teaching. Tape-recording one's own work is at first a frightening experience because there seems to be no place to hide. We feel ourselves naked and exposed. With experience we do not become less naked; we can become more comfortable with our nakedness. In time many teachers are willing to share their tapes with the entire group. Group members usually express their thoughts about a tape with judgment and care. Sharing their experiences in this way leads to further exploration of their own styles of teaching.

A tape recording of one of his classes can often lead the teacher to his own solution to a problem. It permits him to listen with far greater objectivity to the evolution of the teacher-student relationship. The following anecdote is an interesting example of how the recording can help:

During the course of his teacher training, a teacher became concerned about the apathy of one of his classes. He was teaching two sections of the same course, and for a long time couldn't understand why so many students in Section A were uninvolved and not working. At the suggestion of his supervisor, the teacher listened to recordings of the first meetings of both sections, hoping to find a clue as to how he might have influenced this development. There were a number of athletes in Section A—the only obvious difference between the sections. Listening to the recording of Section A he heard his taped voiced giving clear directions to read three books. Then, to his amazement, he heard himself mumbling as an aside that of course the students didn't really have to read anything if they didn't want to.

In thinking about this, he realized that while he was teaching he heard himself giving clear and unambiguous instructions and he experienced the uncomfortable feeling that he was being authoritarian; hence his mumbled aside. This aside compromised his standards of excellence, which had earned him the reputation of being a top-notch teacher. He also realized that his expectations for this group of students were different than for those in Section B. He did not expect athletes to be interested scholars, yet he wanted to be seen as a good joe. The students detected their teacher's ambivalence and chose to honor the impulse that required less effort on their part.

For this teacher, "authoritarian" teaching was uncomfortable and unjustifiable. Although unaware of it at the time, he had equated giving clear instructions with being authoritarian. (As a student he had had a tyrannical teacher, and when he began to teach he resolved to avoid this kind of teaching at all cost.) When he recognized that his assumption had probably contributed to student apathy, the teacher began to think through the assumption again and decided that giving clear instructions might not be authoritarian and tyrannical after all. On the contrary, it might be a clearer expression of trust in the capacity and willingness of his students to learn.

THE IMPLICATIONS OF CONSENSUS

In these discussions, seeking and reaching consensus as an end in itself becomes irrelevant. The teachers are encouraged by the leader neither to seek nor to avoid consensus, because the emphasis is upon individual learning rather than group agreement. From time to time consensus does arise spontaneously among several or all members in the group. The leader can acknowledge its appearance without evaluating it by making such comments as, "A number of you seem to agree that. . ." For example, the group might agree that "unless we listen carefully to students we will not be able to understand where they are in their thinking about the material under discussion." As discussion continues from a point of consensus, it often becomes evident that participants may agree with a general statement, but that the statement has different meanings for the various individuals. In the example just cited, consensus on the importance of listening leaves open for each participant the question of how to listen and what to listen for.

I find that whenever consensus begins to become an end in itself rather than a beginning, certain behavior tends to become defined as legitimate. If at this point a completely contradictory or incongruent position is introduced as another possibility, the participants will tend not to hang onto the consensus as a structure or as a final truth. Otherwise, consensus tends to bring thinking to closure; people accept the consensus as probably the most—and often the only—appropriate way to respond. Consensus can also become directed toward maintaining a certain level of equilibrium as an end rather than as a phase in the process of realization.

As a group proceeds, however, another consensus often begins to make its appearance—an understanding that reflects the participants' developing contract to make this group a place where they can explore their attitudes and assumptions about learning and teaching.

THE VALUE OF ANXIETY

In the first meetings, anxiety is sometimes high. It is important for the supervisor to acknowledge the presence of anxiety, and to encourage participants to talk about the ways they feel anxious, either about their own teaching or about the group discussion itself. Unacknowledged anxiety tends to sustain itself and even to burgeon. As participants acknowledge their own anxiety and become aware that it is appropriate and not unusual, the anxiety generally diminishes. And, having coped with initial anxiety, members learn ways to cope with it when it reappears.

Anxiety often reflects some of our deepest values, and value conflicts. Sometimes anxiety reflects our most profound unexamined values. We fear viewing our most cherished values from a different perspective. Through acknowledging anxiety we can begin to recognize our unexamined values. When anxiety is understood as something through which we can find meaning, the sources of anxiety become the focus of consideration, and anxiety itself seems to wane. When we panic in the face of anxiety or try to ignore it, we sometimes miss the opportunity to understand its source.

In her social studies class, a teacher found herself periodically experiencing feelings of tension. She noticed that these feelings of anxiety usually occurred whenever the class discussion touched on current civil rights issues. There were several black students in her class, whom she tended to avoid calling upon or even looking at during such discussions. She explained that she felt if she invited them to participate she might be viewed as singling them out, whereas if she ignored them she might be protecting them, not trusting their ability to cope with their feelings and to contribute to the learning of the class. She had always considered herself an accepting person, and valued open-mindedness highly. Sharing her classroom experience with the group, she gradually came to realize that her belief in her own open-mindedness was a way of not facing directly a lack of trust in her own ability to cope with human pain and personal embarrassment. Her discomfort in situations that exposed feelings of pain, anger or humiliation, as the class discussions threatened to do, clashed with her belief in open-mindedness. The anxiety which was a result of this conflict enabled her to reflect more deeply on her feelings and values and on the way she expressed them in her teaching.

Sources of Anxiety

Among the sources of anxiety in a group are frustration, the clash of unarticulated discrepancies and the anticipation or experience of actual blows to one's integrity. A participant may feel frustration in a group if he is unable to communicate a deep feeling or belief to the others. As a participant idealizes about learning and teaching, he may become embarrassed by his own limitations and biases. He may experience discrepancy between former beliefs and emerging beliefs. At times he yearns to be told how best to teach, to avoid the frustration of groping and the feeling of being in limbo.

Anticipating or experiencing shame seems to arise in the following kinds of group situations: apprehension before the first meeting (What will it be like? Will my inadequacies as a teacher and as a person be laid bare? Will I have a chance to express my convictions fully? Will they like me and accept me? Will I be able to hold my own?); wondering how widely one's comments during discussion will be broadcast and fearing that one's comments could affect one's job and reputation; not having previously realized certain implications and consequences of one's actions and statements; believing or finding oneself unheard or misunderstood, especially when one has honestly endeavored to communicate.

This is by no means an exhaustive list of anxiety-provoking

situations. It does suggest the variety and intensity of experiences of anxiety. When such experiences are explored directly by participants, anxiety can become a vehicle for learning. Of course, the leader no more attempts to create anxiety-provoking situations than he does to deny or demean anxiety when it does occur.

Acknowledgement of feelings is crucial not only to the functioning of the group, but also to teaching. Too often teachers believe that they should not experience strong emotion in the classroom. Anger, anxiety, fear, helplessness—even joy—seem to have no place there. A fundamental purpose of supervision is to help teachers identify and acknowledge their feelings. If they do not do so, their teaching effectiveness is hampered. A teacher talking in a group session about an event in his classroom is generally able, if we ask him, to tell us quite clearly how he felt at the time of that event. Acknowledging his feelings is the first step toward freeing him to be able to understand the possible sources of those feelings, and to grow in his ability to be aware of the impact his feelings can have on his teaching. If he is able to recognize his feelings as they occur, the teacher can respond more directly and openly, thus offering his students the opportunity to be freer in their participation.

ENCOUNTERING LIMITS

At times, a teacher seems to reach a point in his explorations when he feels he can go no further. He feels he has exhausted his own knowledge about an area of speculation. At the same time, an individual may feel he has reached limits of a more personal sort if his experiences and his capacity to fantasize, to empathize or to identify yield no new meaning or definition of a situation. The social studies teacher caught in conflict between her feelings and her values may feel keenly that she has reached limits within herself. Although she may come to realize the nature of the conflict, she may feel incapable of resolving it or moving into a different relationship with her students and changing her classroom behavior. Feeling the limitations of her own person, she may lose touch both with the feelings and concerns of her students and with her own resources as a concerned, sympathetic teacher.

When this encountering of limits occurs, I find myself considering how I, as leader, can respond so as to help the teachers transcend the limits they are experiencing in the moment. As Jessie Taft (1933) points out, the extent to which we live fully depends upon the extent to which we accept life "on the terms under which it can be obtained, that is, as a changing, finite, limited affair, to be seized at the moment if at all" (p. 13). Taft is referring to a two-person therapeutic relationship, but her observation is no less relevant for other relationships, including supervision. It is often by acknowledging and accepting our limits that we are freed to move beyond them.

When these moments of felt limits occur, participants begin to speculate, "Well, this is as far as we've gone; perhaps it's as far as we can go." Everyone seems to feel in these moments as if they have exhausted their resources. Often, though, someone in the group will come forth and say, "Well, gee, if we look at it from a different position, where can we go?" or "If we take these other things into account, then where does it lead us and how do we move beyond?" In the early meetings, it is sometimes I myself who make such a statement; later, members come quite naturally to respond with this kind of flexibility.

The recognition and acceptance of felt limits poses an irresistible challenge to move on. With the acceptance seems to come an impetus to transcend temporary limits so as to make the most of what Jessie Taft calls "the limited affair of life." The full impact of the group's creative potential finds expression in moments when each participant is able to recognize "where I am now" in the process of his efforts to extend the limits of his learning.

When the participants' felt limits are unacknowledged,

they seem to hold on to them as though moving beyond were impossible. If their felt limits are in any way demeaned, they sometimes clutch them without any apparent desire to move on. Their defensiveness appears to result from experiencing the limits they feel as blatantly revealing and unacceptable. To define the defensiveness as an expression of withdrawal, dogmatism, prejudice or stubbornness only serves to intensify entrenchment. No person with any sense of dignity will risk further sharing when defined in such terms. The acknowledgment and acceptance of limits is an acknowledgment of our own humanity. For these reasons I feel that my initial response to the communication of felt limits is vitally important to the viability and creativity of the group as well as to the learning of each individual.

USE OF THE GROUP EXPERIENCE

The experience of sharing openly with one's colleagues helps teachers begin an internal dialogue that continues after supervision has ended. Such imagined conversations become possible through discovering the multiple perspectives from which any concern or issue can be seen. Ultimately the teacher must act from his own position, out of trust in himself. By imagining dialogues with others in the group, the teacher comes to his own decision with a fuller recognition of the implications and consequences of his actions and with a richer repertoire of address than he might have had without supervision.

A supervisor assumes that the group members possess rich personal resources. He does not at the outset know what particular resources each person has, but he trusts each individual's capacity, given the opportunity, to realize these resources and to bring them to bear on his own teaching. He understands that each person will, in the end, create his own meaning out of his teacher training and his teaching experiences, and he also knows that communicating with colleagues can facilitate and enrich this process. He encourages teachers to explore the meaning to them of their educational ideals and teaching experiences and, in this exploration, to listen attentively to one another. Individuals will want to try various styles of address and to alter their way of responding from time to time during the course of supervision. The supervisor does not attempt to determine a teacher's final stance, but he does expect that various stances will be fully considered, with serious attention given to their implications and consequences for student learning.

Because most teaching takes place in classrooms with a number of students, supervision in a group can provide opportunities for teachers to clarify their assumptions about learning as it occurs in groups and to develop further sensitivities and skills appropriate to group process. In short, the group experience can foster discussion directly relevant to classroom teaching.

THE SUPERVISOR'S JOB

It is frequently assumed that supervisors oversee and evaluate, teachers teach and students learn; that the expectations and processes reside in and are defined by the position or "role." Knowledge and wisdom may be attributed exclusively to the "role" of the supervisor, and institutional expectations and pressures may make a supervisor feel obligated to maintain that stance even though he believes quite differently. The struggle of the supervisor to maintain his status vis-à-vis the group can inhibit the central task of learning through sharing, exploring and challenging the assumptions of the leader— using him as a resource rather than an authority.

If one-to-one supervision is the only kind available to a teacher, he may react to his supervisor either by accepting all that he suggests, or by rejecting without examination whatever he says. It is worth noting that, after an experience in supervision with others, the teacher is more likely to consider a variety of perspectives within the one-to-one relationship; a polarity of views between supervisor and teacher is less likely to occur. Being forced to defend one's status as a supervisor or to defend one's position as a teacher becomes less necessary to save one's sense of dignity.

In discussions, the supervisor serves as a catalyst to learning. He may be an expert in certain areas of teaching and curriculum. He has probably been successful as a teacher and discovered approaches which work well for *him*, but he does not expect the teachers with whom he is working to imitate his style. He uses his expertise in ways that challenge the teachers to exercise their judgment and their capacity to make meaning. Because the supervisor has come to realize through experience an effective teaching style for himself, he trusts each teacher with whom he works to do the same for himself. From time to time, he may share a perspective or a technique but, on the whole, what he shares he offers as only one way of examining emotional and intellectual assumptions about learning and teaching.

SUMMARY

It is not without condition that I advocate supervision in groups. At times individual supervision of teachers is more appropriate. Sometimes an individual conference is the most profitable and fitting response to certain kinds of institutional demands, such as observation and evaluation. Also, supervisor and teacher may find a one-to-one session most suitable for working together on such specific problems as the influence of the teacher's highly personal problems on his teaching, instances of intense teacher upset or situations calling for immediate action. Some teachers seem to learn best from individual supervision. When this appears to be the case, such differences of individual response are worthy of discussion in the group because of their implications for classroom teaching.

The focus in this chapter has been on exploring the ways

the context created in a group relates to the teachers' learning. The fundamental responsibility of supervisors—and teachers, for that matter—is to become aware of the context they create in their effort to help students learn.

The essence of the teaching-learning process is interpersonal. The relationship established between the supervisor and teachers serves as the vehicle through which communication and, hence, learning take place. The nature of the relationship is reflected in the way we respond: that is, what kinds of questions we ask and how we ask them; the way we listen; what we choose to respond to, and our response. To put it simply, the way we teach reflects our beliefs and assumptions about how and why students learn. To understand the complex process of learning requires continuous intensive study. Out of respect for that process I have tried to share some insights from my work with teachers. My hope is that through sharing with teachers both one-to-one and in groups we will increase our professional ability to serve the student in his learning.

CHAPTER EIGHT

NEW DIRECTIONS AND
NEW LEADERS FOR SUPERVISION

Those entrusted with leadership responsibilities in public education confront a series of ideological and social dilemmas posed by their various and often conflicting constituencies. Educators' primary responsibility is the formal instruction of children. They are legally responsible to, and paid by, the community and the parents. Inevitably, individuals develop attachments to a particular school system, a single school or even a particular grade level or department. In addition, many educators feel a deep identity with the profession of teaching and with a special or academic field. Educators are also responsible to themselves as human beings. Thus the supervisor as an educational leader is a person, a citizen, an agent of the society, a teacher, a historian or a mathematician and a member of the staff of, say, Smithville High School. These multiple identifications and conflicting loyalties compound the difficulties posed by the basic educational issues of change versus stability and active leadership versus passive acceptance of change. The issue, for the writers, is construing the role of the supervisor as an active leader of society rather than as an administrative officer who executes educational policy determined by others. It should be clear from preceding chapters that we see this dilemma not as a rigid dichotomy but as a matter of emphasis and orientation. Our position on this question will be discussed later in the chapter.

In order to clarify the leadership dilemmas which confront supervisors (and other educators as well), let us look in some detail at what we consider the two most essential questions confronting education: the organization of the schools for instruction and the nature of the school curriculum. Both issues focus on the problem of leadership.

Let us first deal with the organization of the school for instruction and, more particularly, with the teacher's role.

CONFLICTING VIEWS OF THE TEACHER

There are currently two major views of the role of the teacher, views which are in a certain sense contradictory. On the one hand, there is a powerful movement to professionalize the teacher, increase the status and rewards of teaching and, at the same time, upgrade the quality of training for teachers. On the other hand, however, is a virtually unpublicized trend toward deemphasizing the importance and autonomy of the teacher. We will comment on each of these trends separately.

THE TEACHER AS PROFESSOR

The movement to improve the status of the teacher is, we believe, based on an implicit analogy between the teacher and the university professor. The model is a learned and wise person, steeped in a subject area and in teaching technology and endowed with acute sensitivity to the needs of children. The goal is that every classroom be under the direction of a highly trained, responsible, self-generating, autonomous career teacher. This widely-held vision of The Teacher as Professor can be explained in several ways:

1. The continual upgrading of certification standards is dramatically illustrated by New York and California's insistence on a master's degree or five collegiate years as a prerequisite for permanent certification. In addition, certification requirements are placing greater emphasis on subject matter training and less on professional education courses, in the belief that this constitutes upgrading.

2. Trends in teacher training institutions also reflect the view of the teacher as professor. The increasing popularity of Master of Arts in Teaching and fifth- and sixth-year programs and the rise of internship arrangements are one manifestation. Whereas some ten or so years ago there was much debate over the validity of a fifth-year program, considerable doubt is now cast on the value of undergraduate training programs. Another manifestation is the rising standards of teacher training institutions, as reflected in both the admissions standards of Master of Arts in Teaching programs and the grade-point average required by undergraduate schools as a prerequisite to admission to student teaching.

3. Many school systems seem to operate with this model of the teacher. Certainly, schools are looking hard for teachers with higher academic qualifications. And they are getting them: in 1963, 65% of all teachers had bachelors' degrees as compared to 44% in 1948, and 25% had masters' degrees as compared to 15% in 1948.

4. The various professional organizations have been working hard to increase teachers' status and responsibilities. The National Commission for Teacher Education and Professional Standards in particular has striven mightily to establish professional boards to regulate the profession. And the National Education Association and the American Federa-

tion of Teachers have worked hard and often militantly to improve the teacher's professional and social position as well as his power and dignity.

These, then, are some of the components of the trend toward a teacher in the image of the university professor—a person of status, competence, power and, above all else, autonomy. It is responsible autonomy that is the essential and crucial characteristic of a professional.

THE TEACHER AS TECHNICIAN

At odds with this vision of the teacher as an autonomous professional are several developments which directly and seriously subvert teacher autonomy by implicitly assuming that teachers are not up to the job and that specific measures must be taken to compensate for their deficiencies. A logical extension of this position defines teaching as a technical operation best undertaken with sophisticated educational technology under the direction of an educational technician.

The Curriculum Reform Movement

Perhaps foremost among these developments is the recent spectacular curriculum reform activity, particularly in the development of curriculum materials. This phenomenon has two major aspects—the plethora of curriculum projects like the Physical Science Study Committee, School Mathematics Study Group and Biological Sciences Curriculum Study, and the entrance of giant businesses like International Business Machines, Time, Inc. and Xerox into the field of curriculum materials.

The various new curricula have brought vitality, freshness and imagination to the educational scene. They are typically developed by highly talented people, often dominated by university-connected scholars. Some of the packaged curricula contain a wide range of materials, including films, tapes, readings, programmed instruction tests and the like (and, of course, a teacher's manual). These curricula have usually been undertaken because their developers deplored the existing materials and had little or no confidence that the schools or educators themselves could or would make serious changes.

That these curricula are generally of higher quality than existing materials should be no surprise, since they represent the result of a very substantial investment of talent, time and money. And that is the point. The traditional method—giving a limited number of teachers a limited time (usually a six-week summer workshop) and limited funds—of developing materials is simply no match for a multimillion-dollar project involving some of the best minds in the country.

Packaged materials by their very excellence tend to reduce the autonomy of the individual classroom teacher. It is true that traditional textbooks and courses of study also have a limiting effect on the teacher's freedom. And teachers certainly need materials. Our concern is the degree of the teacher's freedom to determine what and how he teaches, viewed as a continuum at one end of which is the teacher free to do as he wishes and whose opposite pole is the teacher under full constraint. Our opinion is that the current curriculum packages move the typical teacher's role further along the continuum toward constraint and reduced autonomy. Some of the curriculum packagers even talk of producing "teacher-proof" materials.

The point here is not to disparage packaged curricula. Quite the opposite; they should be much better than what has existed before. But it should be pointed out that their very strengths threaten to undermine the role of the teacher (*and* the school *and* the profession) in determining curriculum.

The Education Business

Even more significant for the future is the entrance of Big Business into the picture. Many major companies are attempting to organize a panoply of curriculum-making capacities—film, television, publishing and programmed instruction. These companies mean business, in every sense of the word. They are interested in developing full systems of educational materials to reach the widest possible market. It has been predicted that some of these companies will institute nationwide systems of private schools or under contract to public schools in which fully-integrated, twelve-year-sequenced materials will be tried out and adopted. This development could offer many benefits to education, but it seems likely that only the bravest and hardiest (or richest) of existing schools will be able to resist such competitive pressures.

Educational Television
Other forces, too, threaten to put more and more distance between key curriculum decisions and the teacher. The use of educational television has, *at least up till now*, put the teacher in the position of reacting to a canned presentation in which very few, if any, teachers have actually participated.

Governmental Involvement
The increasingly significant role of the federal government in education and the movement toward larger school districts will probably accentuate this trend. Federally-financed research and development centers will undoubtedly develop and disseminate new curriculum packages, while regional and state agencies will also be stepping up efforts to provide central services.

Reorganization Efforts
Another important and related movement, still in a relatively early phase, is attempting to reorganize the school structure and the teacher's role. It is characterized by such approaches as team teaching, large-group instruction and the development of paraprofessional positions. These reforms, implicitly or explicitly, reflect a view that the schools are not efficiently

organized and the individual classroom teacher needs supplemental help to do his job. An important aspect of team teaching and large-group instruction is their emphasis on cooperative planning and teaching, which can mean a further diminution of the individual teacher's freedom. It may be minimal and may result in better teaching, but it can be a restriction on the individual teacher.

What all this adds up to, in our view, is a very sensible and reasonable recognition that the teacher, as he is now, has not done the job and needs a great deal of help, and that helping involves making better use of the available resources. The trend toward less local control, less teacher autonomy, more curricular coordination (and standardization) and more centralization will undoubtedly increase efficiency and will very probably lead, at least in the short run, to better education for children. There is a price, however: the vision of the teacher as a professor, a self-generating, autonomous person of wisdom and knowledge with full professional responsibilities. A further price may be the initiative, creativity and imagination that grow out of independence and autonomy. And, in a very real sense, these reforms may cost us our vision of a different kind of school and a different kind of professional leader.

NEW TEACHERS AND OLD REALITIES

What are the implications of these conflicting forces for teacher training certification practices and school organization? Should we be training teachers as quasi-professors or as quasi-technicians? By far the more appealing vision, to the writers, is that of the teacher–professor. We believe strongly that autonomy and self-direction are necessary ingredients of creativity. What gives us pause about this vision, however, is recognition of the other necessary ingredient—talent. The fundamental weakness in the argument for "every teacher a professor" is the shortage of available talent. There are now about 2-1/4 million teachers in America; by 1975 we shall probably need almost 3 million. Is it possible to find that magnitude of talent? It is doubtful!

Other requirements need to be met to fulfill the dream of the professor. Teaching conditions would have to improve drastically to allow talent to be fully expressed. Instead of 150 students, a teacher, for example, might be responsible for 30; instead of teaching 25 hours per week, he might teach 10. The basically autocratic structure of the schools would have to be changed to allow teachers freedom to experiment, to inquire broadly and to discharge such research and development responsibilities with imagination and professional integrity. The schools would have to be run by teachers rather than by bureaucrats.

We would need to be considerably more flexible about certification requirements—their complete abolition might be a reasonable start. Since the biggest barrier to staffing the schools with professors is the difficulty of recruiting talent, and since certification laws are widely perceived as nuisances rather than standards, it might be best to leave teacher training exclusively to the universities and schools. If the schools are serious about hiring talented teachers, the universities will respond to their pressure. Certification laws tend to be narrowing and constricting; the image of the professor suggests diversity, brilliance—even eccentricity—qualities which are not encouraged by formal requirements.

This kind of teacher–professor would need lots of training and, more importantly, lots of "education with a small e." Of course, the teacher–professor should have a liberal education of the kind that enlarges a person's humanity. He should have insight into the purposes and traditions of education, a thorough and profound grasp of the content of his field and a full understanding of the teaching–learning process. We will return shortly to a discussion of his role and training; our purpose here is simply to suggest the kind of person we have in mind.

On the other hand, our realistic opinion is that, as exciting, noble and beautiful as this vision is, we cannot expect to find or afford a large number of teacher–professors. Let us, then, face reality, swallow hard and gear up to train two million technicians and a few hundred thousand teacher–professors who can make major curriculum and instructional decisions and train the technicians to implement these decisions. Let us take full advantage of the developing educational technology and of central resources. Much of the day-to-day teaching could be handled by machines or by well-programmed materials administered by technicians. The routine work now handled by teachers could be undertaken by clerks, college students or parttime workers. The manpower needs for such a plan or organization are reasonable, since the ability needed by most technicians corresponds with that of the bulk of the population. Such a personnel and organizational plan would free the teacher–professors to be imaginative and creative, and to attend to their major responsibility—the adaptation or development of the curriculum and the training of the technicians.

NEW CURRICULA AND NEW REALITIES

But new personnel and new organizational plans for education are only half a loaf. *New curricula are equally essential.* We have already contended that public education pays a high price for letting PSSC or Xerox "do it." Our basic argument for new curricula, however, is the stagnation of the present school curriculum. The public school program has not changed fundamentally since education became compulsory in the nineteenth century. The emphasis is still on formal academic work, almost always made up of "courses" in five academic areas—English, science, mathematics, history and foreign languages.

We have noted, in Chapter Two, other forces which have contributed to this emphasis on formal academic work. Specifically, we referred to the public's belief in the necessity of a college education, which, combined with the conservatism of the colleges and the timidity of the schools, has made the school curriculum a prisoner of traditional college entrance requirements. Such factors militate strongly against a consideration of fundamentally different curriculum ideas. We also discussed the Sputnik-era attacks on the schools for their intellectually-deficient offerings and the resultant expensive and hasty efforts to produce better curricula in the sciences, mathematics and foreign languages. We have no quarrel with these curricula—which undoubtedly contribute to effective learning of their subject areas—or with this kind of systems maintenance activity *per se.* But the improvement of existing courses undeniably diverts energy away from a massive and profound reappraisal of the total curriculum. Recent educational developments have tended to add cement to the existing curriculum structure. Such innovations as team-teaching, large-group instruction, television teaching, modular scheduling, computer-aided instruction, and the like are changes *within* the existing curricular frame. Almost all represent better and more efficient ways of teaching the five basic discipline areas. The cupboard of valid alternative modes of education is shockingly bare. What has been called a "revolution" in education is actually reform of the type that maintains the existing system.

The sterility and rigidity of the curriculum has other consequences which argue for change. Academic and psychological pressures on high school students are excessive. They are increasingly questioning the relevance of their education; student cynicism, alienation and militancy constitute the material of headlines.

The perpetuation of the educational status quo is doubly remarkable in an era of unprecedented social and cultural change and turmoil. The nation faces enormous difficulties engendered by racial conflict, war and an increasingly urban society. In the midst of these problems sits the educational system, serenely concentrating on five subject areas and college admissions. Nowhere is leadership in devising alternative forms of education less evident than among professional educators.

Are we tarring supervision with the same brush? The answer is yes. What, then, *is* the supervisor's role in dealing with these issues? Indeed, is it realistic to expect that the typical supervisor, who has spent his professional life trying to improve, say, history teaching, will seriously question whether history should be taught, or that a school principal will reconsider whether schools are a valid place for educators to spend their time? Can we expect incumbents to ask questions and propose answers that threaten their own ideological and professional identities? It is a very real question whether someone deeply immersed in a particular setting is constitutionally able to hypothesize fundamentally different settings. We have also talked about the limitations that can result from the subtle personal and professional ties that accrue during a career. (We suspect that it is these areas that will yield answers to the question of why so little has changed in education.) The innovations we are arguing for would require vast changes in the school's structure, and would undoubtedly be met with bitter and understandable resistance. Is this to ask too much from a supervisor?

NEW LEADERSHIP

It is a basic thesis of this book that there is a compelling need in public education for people able to design and develop curriculum and to analyze teaching. We believe that undertaking these functions could greatly enhance the professional significance and power of what has traditionally been called "supervision." That public education have such leadership is obviously more important than what we call it. Indeed, the term "supervisor" probably has too many negative connotations to survive. We prefer to call these curriculum and instructional leaders "clinical professors." (We are concerned that the reader distinguish between the clinical supervisor, as described in Chapter Five, and the clinical professor. The former is essentially a teacher trainer, who teaches teachers about the curriculum and how to teach it. The clinical professor is able to do this and more.) *What, more specifically, do we envision such leaders doing?*

THE CLINICAL PROFESSOR

The term "clinical" suggests to us *a particular way of achieving practical knowledge about education*. We believe that the most fruitful avenue to the improvement of teaching is the application of the inquiry skills of scholarship to curriculum instruction and formal learning as it actually occurs in the lives of students. The focus of such study is at the point of practice, in schools as well as other educational institutions. Clinical research focuses on the collection of systematic applied knowledge about various curricula, their implementation and effect on different types of students; knowledge about teaching methods, and applied knowledge about students and the way they learn under various conditions of content and instruction. The controlling ideas and hypotheses of clinical research would be the results of the researcher's intensive experience with curriculum, teaching and the students being taught. Thus, reciprocation between thinking about, acting on and researching questions of curriculum, teaching and learning is at the heart of the clinical approach. Clinical research is not oppositional to careful research design or to statistical treatment. Its essential object is to advance our practical knowledge of the complex relationships among curriculum, teaching and student learning.

A clinical professor is thus neither an adjunct professor nor a "master teacher" whose professional job is exclusively to train other skilled teachers. He should have training and competence in the analysis of teaching at least to the degree suggested by Chapters Four through Seven. He is, further, a skilled practitioner directly responsible for the instruction of students. Most important, he is also an analytic scholar, capable of designing and developing original methods and materials for school curricula or for the training of teachers, or of implementing and evaluating instructional designs worked out by others. His clinic is the classroom, or wherever instruction is going on. His method is the systematic and critical analysis of practice. His goal is to demonstrate how to deal with problems of curriculum and instruction and, in so doing, to generate new knowledge about teaching (Bolster 1967).

Training New Leaders

How and where would such clinical professors be trained? We have argued previously that there is no quick and easy way to produce master teachers or to develop in-depth supervisory capabilities. We are arguing the necessity of a further dimension of training, in curriculum theory and development. To do this adequately will, in our opinion, require major initiatives by universities, schools and government to create communities or faculties of competent clinicians and research scholars intellectually committed to studying problems of curriculum and instruction. We are further convinced that the effectiveness of clinical training and inquiry can be enhanced if some clinical researchers forego practicing alone to gather into groups or *clinical communities*. Such groups would be based in the schools and would consist of clinical professors, fellows in the arts and sciences, graduate students in education, experienced teachers undertaking in-service training, beginning teachers and "nonprofessional" faculty. Again, the primary activity of this clinical community would be the development, teaching and testing of curriculum in the broadest sense.

Direct experience with such communities at the Harvard Graduate School of Education and analysis of a teaching hospital where a similar arrangement has long been in operation have convinced us that the training of clinical professors is best accomplished in an environment characterized by: 1) the presence of persons who represent a broad spectrum of knowledge, experience and competence, and all of whom see themselves as directly responsible for the instruction of children and its analysis; 2) an attitude of inquiry which considers all assumptions about curriculum, teaching and learning—whether made by clinical professors, teachers or student teachers—challengeable, accompanied by both willingness and desire to have one's work scrutinized by colleagues; 3) the availability of human resources for learning what is known about a problem (i.e., the community is inhabited by a number of well-informed, inquiring professionals); 4) an organizational framework which allows time and opportunity for systematic reflection and research on practice.

These proposals, for the clinical professor as a curriculum and instructional leader, the school as a center of inquiry and joint university—school programs to train clinical professors, are radical and, in the writers' view, powerful solutions to some of the dilemmas we have discussed. They are not unique to this book, although their combination may be; in fact, schools are already operating as centers of clinical inquiry, and clinical training programs of the type outlined above are currently in operation.[1] Thus, the clinical competencies in curriculum and instruction we feel must supplant the flabbiness of traditional supervision, and the training programs to produce such leadership and the schools in which such clin-

---

[1] We have already referred to Hazard's *The Clinical Professorship In Teacher Education* (1967). Robert Schaefer has argued that the school can be a center of applied research in his book, *The School As A Center of Inquiry* (1967). The Pennsylvania Advancement School in Philadelphia, probably one of the most significant experimental schools in the country, is deeply involved in both curriculum development and teacher training. John Adams High School in Portland, Oregon, is organized to carry on, concurrently, teaching of children, curriculum development, professional training and research.

ical personnel could operate, do not exist merely in the writers' imagination.

Let us summarize the argument so far. We believe that the issues of "what," "how" and "where" we educate students must be subject to profound new thinking and experimentation. We argue for new personnel—clinical professors—and new contexts—clinical communities—to speed this process. In the especially critical area of *curriculum*, what would the clinical professor do? What kinds of curriculum might he innovate?

TWO EXAMPLES OF CURRICULAR INNOVATION

As examples of the kind of curricular and instructional activities we encourage, we would like to describe two projects with which the writers are familiar. Both are part of a program at Harvard funded by the Office of Education under its Training of Teacher Trainers (T.T.T.) division. They are presented as examples of ideas at a formulative stage, not as finished models, and are intended to help clarify our notion of the functions of a clinical professor. It should also be pointed out that these projects are being conducted within the existing school structure. (We are also deeply interested in attempts to develop alternative educational modes outside the traditional structure, such as the Parkways Project in Philadelphia.) The two examples we present are projects in ethical and psychological education.

A PROJECT IN MORAL EDUCATION

One of the most crucial current instructional needs, at all levels of education, is ethical or value education. Surely one of the most important functions of education is to clarify ethical issues—to aid us in living valid, worthwhile, humane and meaningful lives. All of us need such an education, and all of us learn in one fashion or another about moral issues.

But, generally speaking, little systematic attention is given to ethical education in the schools. The schools concentrate on verbal facilities and on the acquisition of knowledge in the five sacred areas. Some argue that ethical issues are involved in most, if not all, of these areas. True enough, but if moral issues arise at all, they usually do so only circumstantially, if they happen to occur in the context of presenting the traditional curriculum. There are notable, widely-scattered exceptions, but it is clear that a tragically small amount of energy is being expended on a curriculum which will help students deal with ethical issues (Kohlberg 1966). Let us emphasize that we are not talking about preaching, brainwashing or the imposition of values. What we *are* urging (and what many young people today are yearning for and demanding) is a curriculum which helps people inquire into and clarify the subtleties, complexities and dilemmas involved in ethical issues.

Background and Theory

The 1920's witnessed a great deal of practical and research interest in moral education in the public schools and church groups (Hartshorne and May 1928; Jones 1936). Moral education during this period was conceived of as explanation of the conventional code, exhortation to follow the code and the planning of group or individual activities which would manifest virtue or good works in terms of this code (Jones 1936). Research evaluation of the results of moral education classes was based on tests of moral knowledge (verbal espousal of the conventional code) and increase in honesty or service as experimentally measured. The results of research evaluation were extremely disappointing. These results, in combination both with opposition to verbal indoctrination as an educational approach and with liberal objections to the teaching of religion in public schools (Kohlberg 1967), led to a marked decline in moral education programs.

On the basis of recent research findings, Kohlberg (1966)

has suggested an approach to moral education free of some of the limitations of earlier approaches. His views are based on a developmental theory of stages or levels in the ability to make moral judgments.

According to Kohlberg's schema, moral education should be an attempt to provide an environment which would stimulate growth in the maturity of moral judgment. It has been theorized that growth in the child's moral maturity is a function, first, of the encounter with moral dilemmas with which the child has to cope, and, second, of the exchange of points of view as to how to solve those dilemmas. The theory postulates that such encounters and exchanges create disequilibrium—cognitive dissonance—in the child and that resolution of the disequilibrium is upward in the sequence, i.e., takes the child to a higher stage of moral maturity.

Only a few experimental attempts have been made to stimulate growth in maturity of moral judgment. One was done by Blatt and Kohlberg (1969); the second, a replication and extension of the first, is the subject of an unpublished Ph.D. dissertation by Blatt (1969). Both studies were based on the following reasoning:

[If moral development] passes through a natural sequence of stages, the approach defines the aim of moral education as the stimulation of the next step of development rather than indoctrination into the fixed conventions of school, the church, or the nation. It assumes that movement to the next step of development rests not only on exposure to the higher level of thought, but to experiences of conflict in the application of the child's current level of thought to problematic explorations. In contrast to conventional moral education, the approach stresses:

1) arousal of genuine moral conflict, uncertainty, and disagreement about genuinely problematical situations. (In contrast, conventional moral education has stressed adult "right answers," and reinforcement of the belief that virtue is always rewarded.)

2) the presentation of modes of thought no more than one level above the child's own. (In contrast, conventional moral education

tended to shift from appeals to comprehensible adult abstractions too far above the child's level to appeals based on punishment and prudence which are below the child's level and therefore liable to rejection.) (p. 5)

The initial research involved relatively simple discussions of moral dilemmas. Some were teacher-led and others were "leaderless." The results were positive.

When the results were analyzed it was found that the changes in moral judgment ordinarily occurred in a sequential order of stages, as described in Kohlberg's theory. If a child, say, began at stage two, he would advance to stage three, and so on. Children who began the program at different stages underwent change relative to their initial stage, even though every child in each group was exposed to the same discussions. This is persuasive evidence that these discussions do not indoctrinate children into a particular stage of moral judgment but, rather, stimulate genuine growth.

Present Staff and Program

A group of Harvard faculty and students particularly interested in moral education has been meeting with public school teachers since 1969 to study the theory and research implications of Kohlberg's schema and of other approaches to moral education. Two potential models of moral education which have been developed are briefly summarized below.

The first model, tentatively called "Education for Responsibility" is an outgrowth of work done by Dr. Joseph Lukinsky of Brandeis University. It was postulated that involvement in "helping" activities (assistance in mental hospitals, community development projects, halfway houses, tutoring projects, and the like) would enhance children's sense of responsibility, as manifested in their relationships with other persons, and would lead to greater self-understanding. Among the variables in this model of moral education are the relationship of the work engaged in to the cognitive and affective development of the particular children working, the effects of discussion or no discussion after "helping" experiences on change in the children's attitudes or behavior, and the like. Further exploration of these ideas is underway.

A second model is based on Kohlberg's cognitive–developmental schema of moral judgment and on the experiments of Blatt and Kohlberg. Blatt (1969) has shown that it is possible to stimulate growth in the level of children's moral maturity in a school setting. Two questions remain unanswered, however, by the experimental teaching in schools. First, is the most important factor in producing change the method of discussion or the personality of the experimenter and his relationship to the children? And, second, if there is a method or technique involved in stimulating moral maturity, is it teachable or transmittable to teachers who do not have extensive familiarity with the development of children's moral judgment? These two questions are of crucial significance if a curriculum is to be developed for wide application in the schools.

Implications for Future Work

The goal of all of these models of moral education is to develop curricula which can be used by trained teachers in almost any school with equally positive results. A great deal of work remains to be done in developing such a generalizable curriculum. Some important questions to be asked about the Blatt and Kohlberg model are: what kinds of materials are relevant for what kinds of children? what methods of presentation best engage children's interest in the moral dilemmas and concerns being discussed? what elements should a moral dilemma have for it most effectively and productively to challenge a child's thinking and help move him to a more mature level of moral judgment? and, what are the conditions for a good discussion of moral dilemmas? Because this curriculum is more concerned with the process of change and how to induce it than with imparting information, the development of the curriculum is particularly complex and requires keen naturalistic observation and study. But the promise of a systematic curriculum in moral education is very great.

A PROJECT IN PSYCHOLOGICAL EDUCATION

The current work at Harvard in "deliberate psychological education" has several roots.[2] The first is a critique of typical guidance and psychological services in schools; a second is an appraisal of the unacknowledged but massive psychological education which students experience in schools. M. A. White has described this as the dual problem of "the little white clinic in the little red school."

Background and Theory

Psychological and guidance services are probably unavailable in a majority of American schools. Where they do exist, there is frequently a significant gap between professional rhetoric about these services and the actual role they play in students' lives. Stripped of their myths, such psychological services really perform two functions within the school. The first is to "adjust" students to the institution. By testing, counseling or referral to community treatment agencies, an attempt is made to adjust the underachieving student or the discipline "case" to "normal" functioning in the school. Satisfactory academic achievement and conformity to school codes of acceptable behavior are the real objectives of the treatment. A much more characteristic guidance service is essentially administrative: determining, with the student, what courses he should take or what college he will attend. In mental health terms, these are low-order secondary prevention activities, attending to symptoms rather than causes.

One of the principal jobs of the psychological personnel within a school is, then, to adjust children to the institution. In so doing, they assume that the school is a static norm, and

[2] For a full description of this project, see Mosher and Sprinthall (1970).

rarely acknowledge that the school environment may be the "problem," rather than the individual student. A contributory factor is the separate and often unequal professional status of guidance personnel or school psychologists in relation to teachers and administrators. They occupy a marginal position within the school. Often, too, the psychological training of school guidance personnel is limited; they typically have a significant involvement with only a small proportion (perhaps 15 percent) of all students in school and probably a lower proportional involvement with teachers and parents. In brief, for a majority of the children in our secondary public schools no significant psychological services or education exist.

A second impetus to work in psychological education is recognition of a more general effect and deficiency of the school itself. Attention has recently been directed to various unanticipated psychological consequences of schooling. We refer to the effects of school on the student's attitude toward learning or his motivation, his self-concept and his ability to think independently. Studies of this phenomenon (see Coleman, Friedenberg, Jackson, Grannis, Sprinthall and Mosher) suggest that schools *are* educating students' attitudes, self-concepts and values; that there is a "hidden curriculum" accompanying formal academic instruction which deeply affects the student's psychological development. In an indirect and unacknowledged manner, schools affect how the student sees himself, his competencies, his worth and his prospects as a human being. The school, at minimum, reinforces the self-image with which the child enters school, and often confirms the negative expectations of large groups of children (especially poor black and white children). In short, teachers are, whether they realize it or not, psychological educators. In addition to teaching mathematics or spelling, they often teach children that adults have power and that children are impotent and irresponsible and should be intellectually and personally dependent. Schools value achievement and competitiveness (or cheating), and foster the belief that self-worth is synonymous with academic achievement. This is a harsh critique of the school, but evidence suggests that this hidden curriculum is typically more inimical and psychologically crippling than it is positive and developmental. That these effects of schooling are largely unrecognized (and presumably unintended) is hardly an extenuating factor.

It is encouraging that this hidden curriculum of psychological and social learnings is increasingly being acknowledged. But as it exists it remains a largely hidden and unplanned consequence of how schools are organized and what knowledge and activities are considered most worthwhile. Furthermore, there presently exist few provisions to correct for these negative effects and no formal mechanism (except the little white clinic) for *the deliberate development of positive psychological growth for all children in the school.* It is this that is the essential concern of the psychological education project. Several assumptions underlie this project in psychological education:

1. The project assumes a belief in the value of self-knowledge and of the examined life; this kind of knowledge is important for the individual, it enables him more fully to realize his own potential and humanness and it will affect how he behaves.

2. Personal psychological growth may develop according to a predictable sequence or series of stages. Erik Erikson and others have suggested that such stages exist; Kohlberg's stages of moral development may be analogous to the levels of personal psychological development. An important goal of the research will be to establish whether certain basic psychological processes (e.g., learning to listen to another person, learning to identify feelings and to respond to them, learning to act on behalf of a personal value) can indeed be located on a continuum of development and complexity.

3. Despite two thousand years of arguments for the development of self-knowledge through education, the project assumes that formal schooling has little positive intentional effect on the process of achieving self-awareness. Learning about Macbeth's emotions is not the same as systematically learning about one's own emotions.

4. We assume that psychological or emotional processes, such as perceiving people correctly and efficiently and expressing feelings, can be taught. Learning such processes can contribute not only to the individual's self-understanding and emotional development but also to his understanding of, and ability to relate to, other people. It is *the deliberate development of these processes, by education, which constitutes the main concern of the project.*

5. Personal psychological growth and deliberate psychological education intended to facilitate these processes are both considered subjects which merit careful study. Such research and development could be undertaken as a separate project, but there can be considerable value in doing both concurrently and thus benefitting from the special training and interests of both psychologists and clinical faculty in education.

A Curriculum in Personal and Human Development

The curriculum being developed can be described most simply as a coordinated set of courses in individual and human development to be taught to high school juniors and seniors. Offered as an elective for credit in psychology, the curriculum, to date, has been tried with 10 experimental classes.

Students elect one of a number of "laboratories," or experience-based courses in psychology and the humanities. These include Improvisational Drama, The Psychology of Interpersonal Behavior, a Laboratory in Teaching, a Seminar and Practicum in Counseling, Communication and the Art of the Motion Picture, a Laboratory in Child Development and Child Care. Respectively and in brief, these laboratories involve the student in the exploration, through dramatic improvisation, of his own and others' behavior; intensive experience of the group process in a self-analytic group; teaching in a variety of settings institutionalized mentally retarded children, normal elementary school children and geriatric patients in a mental institution; studying theory and practice of counseling and, under supervision, counseling younger adolescents; the study of several intensely realistic films about adolescents or young adults, and studying the psychology of child development in conjunction with operating a nursery school.

Each laboratory has three main objectives:

1. To teach material from psychology and/or the humanities pertinent to an understanding of individual and human development. The resource material used to study adolescence, for example, includes excerpts from publications by Erikson, Coleman, Keniston and Harvard Project Pathways; units on intelligence and personality testing; contemporary novels of adolescence and autobiography (e.g., *The Cool World* and *The Autobiography of Malcolm X*); biographical films (e.g., "The Loneliness of the Long Distance Runner," "Nobody Waved Goodbye," "Phoebe"); and comprehensive psychological case studies (e.g., Inburn in *The Uncommitted* and several analogous case work-ups specifically developed for this project).

2. To give the student *systematic personal experience and responsibility*—in, for example, teaching, counseling or child care—relevant to his formal studies in psychology or the humanities. To involve the student personally with the issues he is studying—whether it be how human behavior is determined, what is meant by intelligence, how to "mother" children or how to listen to another person and comprehend what he thinks and feels—is the essential "method" of the laboratories.

3. To encourage the student to consider or make conscious what he learns about himself from his formal study and from his laboratory experience. Students learn a great deal about themselves from such experiences as counseling a high-school junior about college admission or teaching mentally retarded children. In the context of this book, the finding that people make very significant personal meaning out of their initial experiences of teaching or counseling will hardly come as a surprise. What is intriguing is that this is as true for adolescents as it is for graduate students.

This work in deliberate psychological education is in the first year of a projected three-year development. The results are tentative but strongly encouraging. The Harvard faculty members are convinced, for example, that the students in the top half of the high-school class are more effective as counselors than is the bottom half of their graduate-level guidance class (and the high school students have had much less actual counseling practice). In summary, the combination of formal study and real tasks for which the adolescent has defined responsibility evokes not only a rigorous approach to psychology but also, and more important, an enhanced sense of competence and a significant personalization of the experience. Sensitive teachers and counselors can help the adolescent forge these new personal competencies and new personal knowledge.

SUMMARY

These examples of basic curriculum innovation bring us back to the question of the function of supervision. Our own opinion is that there is a need and a place for several kinds of educational leadership. The existing school, the traditional curriculum framework and the teacher all need nurturance and further development. The methods of supervision discussed in Chapters Five through Seven contribute to the maintenance and improvement of the existing educational system. Without such innovative approaches to the curriculum and governance of the school, we can envisage a progressive paralysis of much of that system. Such a breakdown manifestly *can* happen here—regardless of whether we are talking about a city high school convulsed by racial strife or a struggle over community control, or about a prestige Ivy League university shut down by a strike protesting R.O.T.C. or the widening of the war in Southeast Asia.

For the writers, however, the *dominant* educational need at present is the development of alternative educational modes. This involves nothing less than the reformulation or reconstruction of the educational system, a task which requires a new kind of educational leader. We have described him as a clinical researcher whose profession it is to reformulate the context, content and the method of children's education. Such a clinician may be the first truly professional educator. The challenge he faces is to develop a vision of a noble society in which free men can live in wisdom and with humanity. From such visions only can a valid curriculum develop. A society which prides itself on pluralism and diversity must, by definition, offer a pluralistic and diversified education. This means that we must have leaders of broad and varying outlook on what constitutes the good man and the good society, and who are interested in translating these notions into appropriate educational patterns. Their perspective must be broader than the confines of materials, group process techniques and school organizations. Our needs are all too apparent, public interest has never been higher and the rank and file of the profession show increasing signs of frustration and despair with existing arrangements. The major factor which is lacking is the hallmark of valid supervision—leadership.

REFERENCES

Allport, Gordon. *Becoming: Basic Considerations for a Psychology of Personality*. New Haven: Yale University Press, 1955.

Amidon, E. "A Technique for Analyzing Counselor-Counselee Interaction." In *Counseling and Guidance: A Summary View*, edited by J. Adams, pp. 50–55. New York: The Macmillan Company, 1965.

Anderson, C. C., and Hunka, S. M. "Teacher Evaluation: Some Problems and a Proposal." *Harvard Educational Review* (Winter 1963).

Anderson, G. J., and Walberg, H. J. "Classroom Climate and Group Learning." *International Journal of the Educational Sciences* 2 (1968): 175–180.

Ausubel, David P. Review of *Toward a Theory of Instruction*, by Jerome S. Bruner. Harvard Educational Review 36 (Summer 1966): 337–340.

Barr, A. S., *et al.* "The Measurement of Teaching Ability." Madison, Wisconsin: Dembar Publications, 1945.

Bar Yam, M. "The Interaction of Instructional Strategies with Students' Characteristics." Qualifying paper, Harvard University, 1968.

Belanger, M. L. "An Exploration of the Use of Feedback in Supervision." Ed.D. dissertation, Harvard Graduate School of Education, 1962.

Bellack, A. A., *et al. The Language of the Classroom*. New York: Teachers College Press, 1966.

Bennington, G. H. "Self-Acceptance Change in Student

Teachers as a Result of Student-Centered University Supervision." Ed.D. dissertation, University of Oregon, 1965.

Biber, Barbara. "Teacher Education in Mental Health." Paper read at the 33rd annual meeting of the American Orthopsychiatric Association, 1956.

Biddle, B. J. "The Integration of Teacher Effectiveness Research." In *Contemporary Research on Teacher Effectiveness*, edited by B. J. Biddle and W. J. Ellena, pp. 1–40. New York: Holt, Rinehart & Winston, 1964.

Blatt, M. "Studies on the Effects of Classroom Discussion upon Children's Moral Development." Ph.D. dissertation, University of Chicago, 1969.

Blatt, M., and Kohlberg, L. "The Effects of Classroom Discussion upon Children's Moral Judgment." Mimeographed. Harvard Graduate School of Education.

Bloom, B. S. *Taxonomy of Education Objectives, Handbook I.* New York: David McKay Company, 1956.

Blumberg, A., and Amidon, E. "Teacher Perceptions of Supervisor–Teacher Interaction." *Administrator's Notebook* 14 (September 1965): 1–8.

Bolster, Arthur S., Jr. "The Clinical Professorship: An Institutional View." In *The Clinical Professorship in Teacher Education*, edited by W. R. Hazard. Evanston, Ill.: Northwestern University Press, 1967.

Brown, A. B.; Cobban, M. R.; and Waterman, F. T. "The Analysis of Verbal Teaching Behavior: An Approach to Supervisory Conferences with Student Teachers." Ed.D. dissertation, Teachers College, Columbia University, 1966.

Brown, R. V., and Hoffman, M. J. S. "A Promissory Model for Analyzing and Describing Verbal Interaction Between College Supervisors and Student Teachers During Supervisory Conferences." Ed.D. dissertation, Columbia University, 1966.

Bruner, Jerome S. *Toward A Theory of Instruction.* Cambridge, Mass.: Harvard University Press, 1966.

——. *On Knowing.* Cambridge, Mass.: Harvard University Press, 1962.

Cogan, Morris L. "Supervision at the Harvard-Newton Summer School." Mimeographed. Harvard Graduate School of Education, 1961.

Conant, James B. *The Education of the American Teacher.* New York: McGraw-Hill Book Company, 1963.

Cremin, Lawrence A. "The Progressive Heritage of the Guidance Movement." In *Guidance: An Examination,* edited by Ralph L. Mosher *et al.* New York: Harcourt, Brace & World, 1965.

——. *The Transformation of the School.* New York: Alfred A. Knopf, 1961.

Deutsch, F. *Applied Psychoanalysis.* New York: Grune & Stratton, 1949.

Domas, S. J., and Tiedeman, D. V. "Teacher Competence: An Annotated Bibliography." *Journal of Experimental Education* 19 (1950): 99–218.

Edelfelt, Roy A. "Educating the New Teacher." *Educational Leadership* 24 (November 1966): 147–150.

Edmund, N. R., and Hemink, L. "Ways in Which Supervisors Help Student Teachers." *Educational Research Bulletin* 37 (March 1958): 57–60.

Fattu, Nicholas A. "Research on Teacher Evaluation." *National Elementary Principal* 43 (November 1963): 19–27.

Flanders, N. A. "Some Relationships Among Teacher Influence, Pupil Attitudes, and Achievement." In *Contemporary Research on Teacher Effectiveness,* edited by B. J. Biddle and W. P. Ellena, pp. 196–231. New York: Holt, Rinehart & Winston, 1964.

Getzels, J. W., and Jackson, P. W. "The Teacher's Personality and Characteristics." In *Handbook of Research on Teaching*, edited by N. L. Gage, pp. 506–582. Chicago: Rand McNally & Co., 1964.

Goldhammer, Robert. *Clinical Supervision: Special Methods for the Supervision of Teachers.* New York: Holt, Rinehart & Winston, 1969.

Guilford, J. P. *Personality.* New York: McGraw-Hill Book Company, 1959.

Gwynn, J. Minor. *Theory and Practice of Supervision.* New York: Dodd, Mead & Co., 1961.

Harris, Ben M. "Strategies for Instructional Change: Promising Ideas and Perplexing Problems." In *The Supervisor: Agent for Change in Teaching.* Washington, D.C.: Association for Supervision and Curriculum Development, 1965.

Hartshorne, H., and May, M. A. *Studies in the Nature of Character.* New York: The Macmillan Company, 1928–1930.

Hazard, William R., ed. *The Clinical Professorship in Teacher Education.* Evanston: Northwestern University Press, 1967.

Heidelbach, R. "The Development of a Tentative Model for Analyzing and Describing the Verbal Behavior of Cooperating Teachers Engaged in Individualized Teaching with Student Teachers." Ed.D. dissertation, Columbia University, 1967.

Hollister, G. E. "The Group Conference of the Supervising Teacher." *Journal of Educational Research* 44 (September 1950): 54–56.

Hough, J. B. "An Observational System for the Analysis of Classroom Instruction." Mimeographed. Columbus: Ohio State University College of Education, 1965.

Hummel, Raymond. "Ego-Counseling in Guidance." In *Guidance: An Examination*, edited by R. L. Mosher *et al.* New York: Harcourt, Brace & World, 1965.

———. "Ego Counseling in Guidance: Concept and Method." *Harvard Educational Review* 32 (Fall, 1962): 463–482.

———. "Ego-Counseling: Concept, Method and Research." Paper read at meeting of the American Psychological Association, New York, 1961.

Ishler, R. E. "An Experimental Study Using Withall's Social-Emotional Climate Index to Determine the Effectiveness of Feedback as a Means of Changing Student Teachers' Verbal Behavior." Ed.D. dissertation, Pennsylvania State University, 1965.

Jones, E. E. "Authoritarianism as a Determinant of First-Impression Formation." *Journal of Personality* 23 (1955): 107–127.

Jones, V. *Character and Citizenship Training in the Public School.* Chicago: University of Chicago Press, 1936.

Knoell, D. M. "Prediction of Teaching Success from Word Fluency Data." *Journal of Educational Research* 46 (1953): 673–683.

Kohlberg, L. "Moral Education, Religious Education, and the Public Schools." In *Religion and the Public Schools,* edited by Theodore Sizer. Boston: Houghton Mifflin Company, 1967.

———. "Moral Education in the Schools: A Developmental View." *The School Review* 74 (Spring 1966): 1–30.

Kyte, G. C. "The Effective Supervisory Conference." *California Journal of Educational Research* 13 (September 1962): 160–168.

———. *How to Supervise.* Boston: Houghton Mifflin Company, 1930.

Leonard, George B. *Education and Ecstasy.* New York: The Delacorte Press, 1968.

Levinson, D. J. "Role, Personality and Social Structure in the Organizational Setting." *Journal of Abnormal and Social Psychology* 58 (1959): 170–180.

Lindemann, Erich. "The Meaning of Crisis in Individual and Family Living." *Teachers College Record* 57 (1956): 310–315.

Lucio, William H., and McNeil, John D. *Supervision: A Synthesis of Thought and Action.* New York: McGraw-Hill Book Company, 1962.

Lukinsky, Joseph. "Education for Responsibility: A Case Study in Curriculum Development." Ph.D. dissertation, Harvard University, 1969.

MacGraw, F. M. "The Use of 35mm Time Lapse Photography as a Feedback and Observational Instrument in Teacher Education." Ed.D. dissertation, Stanford University, 1965.

McConnell, G. "They Helped Us, But—." *Journal of Teacher Education* 11 (March 1960): 84–86.

McDonald, F. J.; Allen, D. W.; and Orme, M. E. J. "The Effects of Self-Feedback and Reinforcement on the Acquisition of a Teaching Skill." Unpublished paper, Stanford University, 1965.

McGee, H. "Measurement of Authoritarianism and its Relation to Teachers' Classroom Behavior." *Genetic Psychological Monograph* 52 (1955): 89–146.

Meux, Milton, and Smith, B. O. "Logical Dimensions of Teaching Behavior." In *Contemporary Research on Teacher Effectiveness*, edited by B. J. Biddle and W. P. Ellena, pp. 127–164. New York: Holt, Rinehart & Winston, 1964.

Molchen, Kenneth J. "A Study of Changes in Intentions, Perceptions, and Classroom Verbal Behavior of Science Interns and Apprentices." Ed.D. dissertation, Harvard Graduate School of Education, 1967.

Morrison, V. B., and Dixon, W. R. "New Techniques of Observation and Assessment of Student Teaching." In *The College Supervisor: Conflict and Challenge*, 43rd Yearbook of the Association for Student Teaching, pp. 96–103. Cedar Falls: The Association, 1964.

Mosher, R. L. "The Process of Supervision in Professional Training: A Survey of Selected Professions." Unpublished special paper, Harvard Graduate School of Education, 1962.

Mosher, R., and Sprinthall, N. "Psychological Education in Secondary Schools: A Program to Promote Individual and Human Development." *The American Psychologist* 25 (October 1970): 911–924.

Moser, J. M. "A Case Study of the Effect of Information Feedback on the Performance of Student Teachers in Mathematics." Ed.D. dissertation, University of Colorado, 1965.

Newmann, Fred M., and Oliver, Donald W. "Education and Community." *Harvard Educational Review* 37 (Winter 1967): 61–106.

Rogers, Carl. "The Interpersonal Relationship: The Core of Guidance." *Harvard Educational Review* 32 (Fall 1962): 416–422.

Rosenthal, Robert, and Jacobson, Leonore. *Pygmalion in the Classroom; Teacher Expectation and Pupils' Intellectual Development.* New York: Holt, Rinehart & Winston, 1968.

Roth, L. H. "Selecting Supervising Teachers." *Journal of Teacher Education* 12 (December 1961): 476–481.

Ryans, D. G. *Characteristics of Teachers.* Washington, D.C.: American Council on Education, 1960.

Schaefer, Robert. *The School as a Center of Inquiry.* New York: Harper & Row, 1967.

Schueler, H. and Gold, M. "Video Recordings of Student Teachers: A Report of the Hunter College Research Project." *Journal of Teacher Education* 15 (December 1964): 358–364.

Schueler, Herbert; Gold, Milton J.; and Mitzel, Harold E. "The Use of Television for Improving Teacher Training and for Improving Measures of Student Teaching Performance. Phase 1. Improvement of Student Teaching." Hunter College of the City University of New York, 1962.

Scodel, A., and Mussen, P. "Social Perceptions of Authoritarians and Non-Authoritarians." *Journal of Abnormal and Social Psychology* 48 (1953): 181–184.

Seager, G. B. "The Development of a Diagnostic Instrument of Supervision." Ed.D. dissertation, Harvard Graduate School of Education, 1965.

Shaplin, Judson. "Practice in Teaching." *Harvard Educational Review* 31 (Winter 1961): 35.

Sprinthall, N.; Whiteley, J.; and Mosher, R. "A Study of Teacher Effectiveness." *Journal of Teacher Education* 18 (1966): 93–106.

Stern, G. G. "Measuring Noncognitive Variables in Research on Teaching." In *Handbook of Research on Teaching,* edited by N. L. Gage, pp. 398–447. Chicago: Rand McNally, 1963.

Swineford, E. "Analysis of Teaching-Improvement Suggestions to Student Teachers." *Journal of Experimental Education* 32 (Spring 1964): 299–303.

Symonds, P. M. "The Improvement of Teaching Through Counseling of the Teacher." *Journal of Teacher Education* 6 (1955): 122–127.

Taft, Jessie. *The Dynamics of Therapy in a Controlled Relationship.* New York: The Macmillan Company, 1933.

Travers, R. M., *et al.* "The Anxieties of a Group of Student Teachers." *Educational Administration and Supervision* 38 (1952): 368–375.

Trimmer, R. L. "Tell Us More, Student Teacher!" *Journal of Teacher Education* 12 (June 1961): 229–231.

Trimmer, R. L. "Student Teachers Talk Back." *Journal of Teacher Education* 11 (December 1960): 537–538.

Walberg, H. J., and Anderson, G. J. "Classroom Climate and Individual Learning." *Journal of Educational Psychology* 59 (1968): 414–419.

Welch, W. W. "Correlates of Course Satisfaction in High School Physics." Harvard University, 1968.

Weller, Richard H. "An Observational System for Analyzing Clinical Supervision of Teachers." Ed.D. dissertation, Harvard University, 1969.

Wright, R. G. "An Analysis of the Techniques of Guiding Student Teaching Experiences." Ed.D. dissertation, University of Southern California, 1965.

Yulo, R. J. "An Exploration of the Flanders System of Interaction Analysis as a Supervisory Device with Science Interns." Ed.D. dissertation, Harvard Graduate School of Education, 1967.

Zahn, R. "The Use of Interaction Analysis in Supervising Student Teachers." Ed.D. dissertation, Temple University, 1965.

224